Rubber Band

BRACELETS

Rubber Band

Band

BRACELETS

35 colorful
projects you'll
love to make

Lucy Hopping

CICO **kidz**

Published in 2014 by CICO Kidz
An imprint of Ryland Peters & Small
519 Broadway, 5th Floor, New York NY 10012
20–21 Jockey's Fields, London WC1R 4BW
www.rylandpeters.com

10 9 8 7 6 5 4 3 2 1

A CIP catalog record for this book is
available from the Library of Congress and
the British Library.

ISBN: 978-1-78249-159-0

Printed in China

Editor: Sarah Hoggett
Designer: Louise Turpin and Alison Fenton
Illustrator: Louise Turpin
Photographer: Terry Benson
Stylist: Rob Merrett

contents

chapter 1

easy-peasy bracelets 18

chapter 2
craftier bracelets 54

chapter 3
awesome accessories 92

introduction

Rubber-band bracelets are the newest crafting craze around—everywhere you turn, people are adorned with bright and funky jewelry creations! This book includes 35 fantastic projects with detailed step-by-step instructions and illustrations, plus loads of extra ideas to inspire you to create your own designs.

Begin with the techniques section and learn how to make your own loom, what materials you will need, and the basics of rubber-band jewelry. Then start off with the Easy-Peasy Bracelets—simple bracelets that look great, but are quick and easy to make. Graduate to the Craftier Bracelets, which are a bit trickier and often require a larger loom. Finally, move on to Awesome Accessories—quirky little projects such as clip-on earrings, key fobs, and charms.

The rubber-band movement began in the US, when an enterprising Dad named Cheong Choon Ng saw his daughters making bracelets from rubber bands. He fashioned a loom for them so that they could make more intricate bracelets rather than just simple threaded single designs. Eventually he started manufacturing these and this became known as the "Rainbow Loom." Since then, many other brands have come into the market—and the rubber-band bracelet craze has exploded!

Rubber-band bracelets are an ideal summer camp or sleepover activity. It's such fun for you and your friends to help each other master a new design and then experiment with different-colored bands to create a unique piece of jewelry or a special gift. Why not make a stash, set up a stall at your school fair, and sell your wares to raise money for the school or a charity organization?

So sit back, open up the techniques section, and get ready for a new and exciting craft to take over your life. You'll soon find that mini rubber bands are finding their way into every nook and cranny of your home. Rubber-band bracelets are here to stay!

tools & materials

Although you can make the simplest of bracelets with only your hands, a few bands, and a clip, most of the projects in this book require a loom and a few extras. In this section we guide you through all the tools you need, where to get them from, and how to use them. There is even an explanation of how to make your own loom.

Looms

The rubber-band projects in this book are mostly made using a loom. However, you can make the most simple bracelet (the Single Bracelet on page 20) with just your hands or a crochet hook. The Butterfly charm on page 103 is also made just using a crochet hook.

At the beginning of each project, we have told you what size loom you will need, whether the pegs should be set up in a square or diagonal format, and what direction the arrows on your loom should be facing.

Making your own loom

You can also make your own loom using a piece of wood, a ruler, some nails or screws, a hammer or drill/screwdriver, and an adult!

To make all the projects in this book, you will need to make two looms—one in the diagonal format and one in the square format. I suggest you make your loom in the bigger size shown here, so that you can make all the projects with just these looms—but you may prefer to start with a smaller 3 x 13 peg loom first.

Making a square-format loom

You Will Need

(to make a large 26 x 6-peg loom)

A piece of wood 19 in. (52 cm) long x 4¹/₄ in. (12 cm) wide and 2 in. (5 cm) thick

Ruler and pencil

156 x 2-in. (5-cm) nails and a hammer (or 156 x 2-in./5-cm screws, a drill, and a screwdriver)

1 Starting on the short end and using a ruler and pencil, make a mark ³/₈ in. (1 cm) in from the edge on both sides. Then mark every ³/₄ in. (2 cm) between those two points so there are six dots, each ³/₄ in. (2 cm) apart.

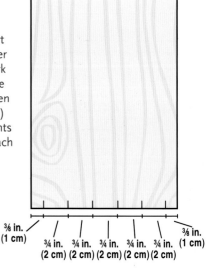

³/₈ in. (1 cm)   ³/₄ in. (2 cm)   ³/₄ in. (2 cm)   ³/₄ in. (2 cm)   ³/₄ in. (2 cm)   ³/₄ in. (2 cm)   ³/₈ in. (1 cm)

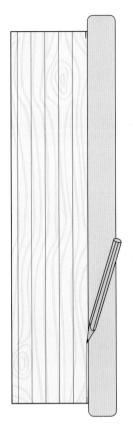

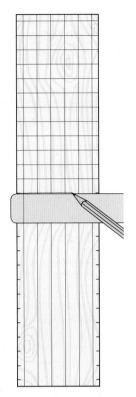

MAKING A SMALL, SQUARE-FORMAT LOOM

To make a smaller 13 x 3-peg loom, take a piece of wood measuring $9^3/_4$ x 3 in. (26 x 6 cm) and repeat the steps above, making three marks along each short side and 13 along each long side.

2 Repeat on the other short end of the loom, then join the marks together so that you have six lines running lengthwise along your piece of wood.

3 Now working along the long sides of the wood, make a mark $^3/_8$ in. (1 cm) in from both sides, then mark every $^3/_4$ in. (2 cm) again. Repeat on the other side, and then join your marks with lines again so you have 26 horizontal lines. The points where the lines meet are where your nails or screws will go.

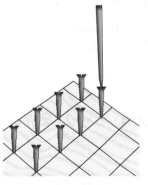

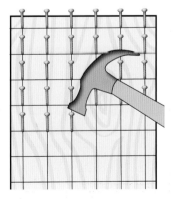

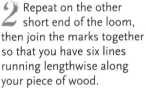

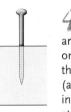

4 Ask an adult to help you with this bit. If you are using nails, hammer in one nail at each point, so that half of the nail (approx. 1 in./2.5 cm) goes into the wood and half is still above the surface of the loom. Repeat at each marked point on the loom.

5 If you are using screws, ask an adult to drill a hole slightly smaller than the diameter of your screw at each point, and then twist the screws into the holes using a screwdriver. Repeat on the whole loom.

Making a diagonal-format loom

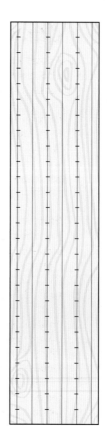

You Will Need

(to make a large 26 x 6-peg loom)

A piece of wood 20 in. (52 cm) long x 4^1/$_4$ in. (12 cm) wide and 2 in. (5 cm) thick

Ruler and pencil

156 x 2-in. (5-cm) nails and a hammer (or 156 x 2-in./5-cm screws, a drill, and a screwdriver)

1 Follow steps 1 and 2 of **Making a square-format loom**, on page 8.

2 On your first vertical line, make a mark ^{3}/$_8$ in. (1 cm) up from the edge of the wood, and then make a mark every ^{3}/$_4$ in. (2 cm) to the top of the loom. You should have 26 marks. Repeat this on alternate lines.

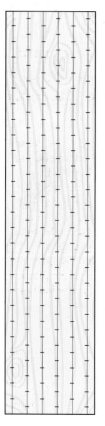

3 On the second vertical line (and every alternate line), make a mark ^{3}/$_4$ in. (2 cm) up from the edge and then every ^{3}/$_4$ in. (2 cm).

4 Add the nails or screws where the lines cross, as in steps 4 and 5 of **Making a square-format loom**.

Note: For projects made on the diagonal loom, it is important that you lay the bands with the loom in the correct direction. Add arrows to the bottom of your loom to help you remember.

MAKING A SMALL, DIAGONAL-FORMAT LOOM

To make a smaller 13 x 3-peg loom, take a piece of wood measuring 10^1/8 x 3 in. (27 x 6 cm) repeat the steps above, making three marks along each short side and 13 along each long side. You may find it easier to shape the bottom of the loom in a point (either by cutting it or drawing it on) so that you always start laying your bands the correct way.

Plastic loom

The most popular type of loom is made from plastic and can be bought from craft stores or online. The benefit of a plastic loom is that it has been specially designed for rubber band bracelets, so you can adapt it to make the layout and size of loom that you need. Most looms are made from three strips of 13 pegs that can be pulled apart and attached together in a square or diagonal layout. You can also buy extra looms and join them together to make wider and longer looms, which is very handy for some of the larger projects.

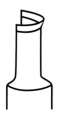

Side view　　**Top view**

Each peg is hollow, so you can insert your hook into it, and has an open back which makes it easy to catch the band in the tip of your hook to loop it over.

Other equipment

As well as your loom you will need a good strong crochet hook, rubber bands, and C-clips to begin making your projects. You may also want to get a collection of beads and charms to add to your designs. Once you have completed your project, you may want to turn it into something—in which case you will need split rings, ring blanks, hairclips, and so on.

Hooks

The looms that you buy from craft stores or online generally come with a plastic hook, but if you are making your own loom or break your hook, use a US size G/6 (4mm) metal crochet hook. It will be much stronger and won't bend when you are working on some of the projects that have a lot of tension in them, such as the Double Braid Bracelet on page 74.

You can also use the thicker end of the hook that comes with ready-made looms to help you prise the strips apart when you need to assemble them in a different format or join two or more looms together to make a loom that's either wider or longer than normal.

Rubber bands

This is where you can let your imagination run wild! There are many different types of bands available, including colored, jelly, neon, glitter, metallic, glow-in-the-dark, and even scented bands! Some bands are better quality and stronger than others, so always try and buy good-quality ones as you will find the cheaper ones snap during the looping and pulling off the loom stages. This is very frustrating!

Try organizing your bands into colors and separating them into a plastic segmented storage box or individual sandwich bags. This makes things much easier, as there is nothing more frustrating than searching for that last elusive pink band to complete your project and not having one!

S-clip　　**C-clip**　　**Locking C-clip**

Clips

Plastic clips are used to secure the last loops in a project together so that it does not fall apart. They come in three main designs—C-clips, S-clips, and locking clips. Locking clips are usually in bright colors, so you can match them to the design of the bracelet or necklace. S-clips and C-clips are generally made from clear plastic, so they are better for use in charms as they cannot be seen.

Beads and charms

Beads and charms can be added to your projects for extra color and texture. Beads need to have a large central hole in them so that a doubled-over band can be threaded through, so plastic pony beads are my preferred choice. They are added to the project during the laying-out stage. See opposite for more information on how to use them.

Special rubber-band charms can be bought which already have plastic clips attached to them. These come in many themes such as flowers, popular characters, animals, and more. They are made from plastic and are simply clipped onto the project after looping.

Jewelry findings

To turn charms into useful accessories such as clip-on earrings, rings, split rings, and keyrings, you will need a good supply of metal jewelry findings. Available in craft stores, online, and in beading shops, these are a really effective way of showing off your creations!

To make hair accessories, try visiting your local supermarket or accessories store for plain hairbands, hair ties, and hairclips. There are a wide range of colors, sizes, and shapes available, so you can match them with the loops you have used for that particular project!

Glue

To attach the jewelry findings to the charms, you will need a glue gun or some superglue. These are both very strong and dangerous glues to use, so ask an adult to supervise you at all times.

A glue gun is a special tool that is plugged in and heats up. When the gun is warm enough, the glue stick in the gun melts and can be squeezed out using the trigger. The glue is very hot when it comes out, so be very careful not to burn yourself. It cools down and hardens very quickly, though, so it is a very speedy way of completing your projects.

Superglue is a clear and very strong chemical glue. It can be bought from craft stores, hardware stores, and online. Do not touch the glue, as it is very sticky and will stick itself to everything. Make sure you read the instructions carefully before you use it.

Felt

Once you have glued your jewelry finding to your charm, the back can look very messy. Small pieces of felt stuck over the back hide all the glue and also add strength to the piece. Craft felt comes in a wide variety of colors, so you can find the perfect one that suits your project.

techniques

There are a few simple techniques to master before you try the projects in this book, such as laying out your bands, hooking them, and finishing off the designs. Read these tips carefully before a project to ensure they are a success and do not fall apart when you pull them from the loom!

Laying out your bands

The first step in making your bracelet is to lay out your bands.

At the beginning of each project, we have put a diagram to show what type of loom set-up you need. Check whether it is a square or diagonal format and adjust or select the correct loom, depending on whether you are using a store-bought or homemade loom.

Usually the bands are laid with the arrows on the loom pointing away from you and the closed side of the pegs facing you.

Lay your bands in the order specified in the instructions. If you do not lay them in the correct order, then when you come to hooking the bands and pulling the project off the loom it may fall

apart or look different to the finished picture.

Always push the bands down on the pegs, especially if there are lots of bands on the pegs. This makes it easier to hook them and also prevents them from falling off the pegs.

Cap bands

A cap band is added to the top of a peg once all the bands have been laid out. This is a band that is twisted around the peg—four times usually—and forms a stopper for the bracelet so that the bracelet does not fall apart when you pull it from the loom. These

bands are not hooked; instead, you pick up the band below the cap band and hook that band over its opposing peg. Cap bands are normally on the last peg of a design or in the center of a hexagonal pattern.

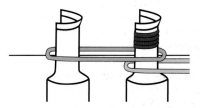

Adding beads

To add beads to a design, you need to add them as you lay your bands out.

1 Before laying the band on the pegs, thread a band through the hole in the bead.

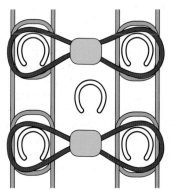

2 Hook the beaded bands over the pegs as normal.

Hooking your bands

Once you have laid out all your bands, you normally turn the loom around so that the arrows on your loom are facing toward you. This means that the open side of the pegs is facing toward you, which makes it easier to get the hook into the peg and to pick up the band with the tip of your hook.

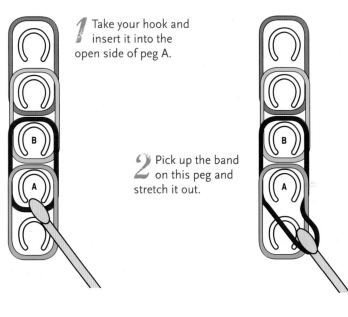

1 Take your hook and insert it into the open side of peg A.

2 Pick up the band on this peg and stretch it out.

3 Now hook the band that you've just picked up onto the peg that the other end of the band is on. This peg may be above, to the side of, or diagonally opposite the first peg. I call this, hooking it over the opposing peg.

Opposing peg (B) is above the first peg (A)

Opposing peg (B) is to the side of the first peg (A)

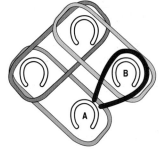

Opposing peg (B) is diagonally above the first peg (A)

4 A teardrop shape is formed, which traps the ends of the previous band so that your bracelet doesn't unravel. Repeat the hooking process in the order shown in your project.

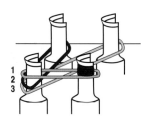

Note: If there are lots of layers of bands in your project, you will work from the top band downward. So you would hook the blue band first, then the red band, and finally the green band.

Pulling your bracelet off the loom

Once all your bands are hooked over, and before you pull them off the loom, double check that you have teardrop shapes between each peg. These teardrops keep all the bands together and stop the bracelet from falling apart when you pull it off the loom.

If you do notice a mistake, you can unhook your bands, working backward in order in the way you hooked them, and fix the mistake before it's too late and you end up with a loopy mess!

Once you are satisfied, insert your hook into the top row of pegs in that design. You may have just one peg or more to insert your hook into. Pick up all the loops

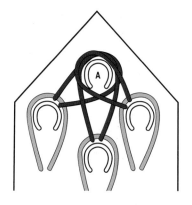

Just one peg on the top row

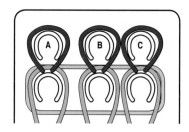

Three pegs on the top row

on those pegs and gently pull the bracelet off the loom. Do not pull too hard or too quickly or the

bands may snap! You should now have a bracelet on your hook.

Extending a bracelet or a necklace

A bracelet made on a single 3 x 13-peg loom is not usually long enough to fit around your wrist or neck. To make it longer, add a chain of bands. This can be done by hooking them with the hook or on the loom.

Hook method

1 With the bracelet loops still on your hook, thread a band onto it and pull one end through the loops on the hooks. Then (using your fingers) put the other end of the band on your hook.

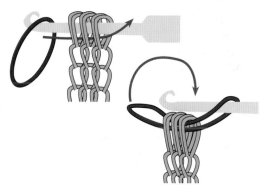

2 You will now have two loops on your hook.

3 Repeat until your bracelet or necklace is long enough (approx. 10 extra bands for a bracelet and 25 for a choker).

4 Finish by inserting the loops on your hook onto a C-clip.

Loom method

1 Keep your bracelet loops on the hook and put to one side.

2 With your loom set up in the diagonal format, 2 pegs wide x 13 pegs long, and with the inverted side facing you, lay out your extension bands as shown (10 for a bracelet or 25 for a choker). Place the loops on your hook on the bottom peg.

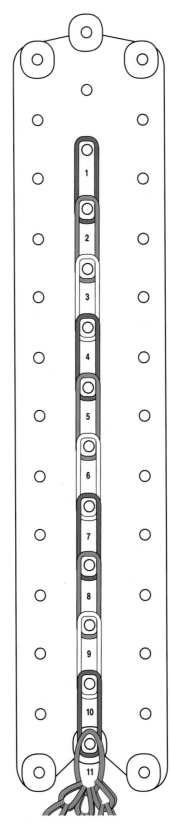

10 extension bands for a bracelet

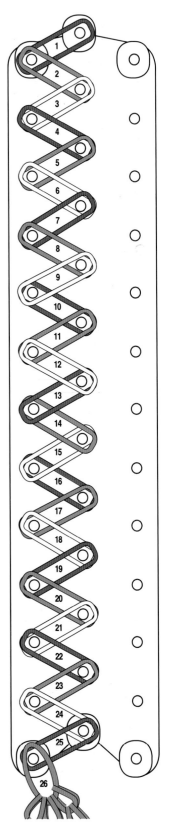

25 extension bands for a choker or necklace

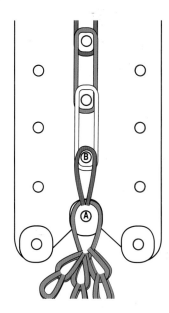

3 Now take your hook, insert it into peg A, and hook the bands over peg B—in the same way as when making a single bracelet using the loom method (see page 20). Repeat all the way up the loom.

4 Insert your hook into the loops on the last peg and pull the bracelet or choker off the loom.

5 Finish by inserting the loops on the hook into a C-clip and attaching the C-clip to the loops at the start of the bracelet or choker.

PRACTICE MAKES PERFECT! DON'T BE DISCOURAGED IF YOUR FIRST ATTEMPT AT A DESIGN DOESN'T WORK OUT—JUST PULL THE BANDS OFF AND START AGAIN!

ALWAYS GET OUT YOUR BANDS BEFORE STARTING A PROJECT. AS WELL AS MAKING THE LAYING-OUT STAGE QUICKER, THIS ALSO MEANS YOU CAN MAKE SURE YOU HAVE ENOUGH OF EACH COLOR TO COMPLETE THE PROJECT!

WHEN LAYING OUT THE BANDS, ALWAYS MAKE SURE YOU HAVE YOUR LOOM FACING THE CORRECT WAY, AS SPECIFIED IN THE INSTRUCTIONS. USUALLY THIS IS WITH THE ARROWS ON THE LOOM FACING AWAY FROM YOU—BUT SOME PROJECTS ARE WORKED THE WRONG WAY AROUND.

ALWAYS LAY OUT THE BANDS IN THE ORDER SPECIFIED IN THE INSTRUCTIONS. A LITTLE MISTAKE CAN RESULT IN A BRACELET THAT DOESN'T HOLD TOGETHER OR LOOKS DIFFERENT FROM WHAT YOU WERE EXPECTING.

PRESS THE BANDS DOWN ON THE LOOM AS FAR AS POSSIBLE, ESPECIALLY WHEN THERE ARE LOTS OF BANDS ON EACH PEG. THIS WILL PREVENT THEM FROM FALLING OFF THE LOOM WHEN YOU ARE HOOKING.

WHEN HOOKING THE BANDS, ALWAYS HAVE THE ARROWS POINTING TOWARD YOU AND, IF YOU ARE USING A PLASTIC LOOM, THE OPEN SIDE OF THE PEGS FACING YOU.

ALWAYS PICK UP THE TOP BAND ON THE PEG (EXCLUDING THE CAP BAND) AND WORK DOWNWARD WHEN LOOPING YOUR BANDS.

BEFORE PULLING YOUR BRACELET OFF THE LOOM, CHECK THAT ALL THE BANDS HAVE BEEN HOOKED AS REQUIRED. THE HOOKING CREATES A TEARDROP SHAPE, AND EVERY BAND SHOULD BE TRAPPED IN ONE OF THESE TEARDROP SHAPES.

chapter 1

easy-peasy bracelets

single bracelets

This is the first type of bracelet for you to try. There are three ways to make it: by hand, with a crochet hook, and on a loom.

SKILL LEVEL ✱

You Will Need

Assorted bands—25 per bracelet

C-clip

Making a bracelet by hand

1 Take your first loop and pinch it flat.

2 Add a C-clip to the center.

3 Flatten your next band and insert it through the loops of the first band.

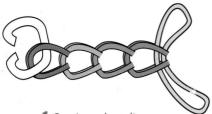

4 Continue threading flattened bands through the previous loops until your bracelet is the length you want (approx. 6 in./15 cm).

5 To complete your bracelet, hook the last two loops through the C-clip at the start of the bracelet.

Making a bracelet with a hook

SKILL LEVEL ✳

You Will Need

Assorted bands—25 per bracelet

C-clip

Hook

1 Follow steps 1 and 2 of **Making a bracelet by hand**, opposite. On step 3, insert your hook into the loops of the first band.

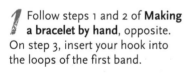

2 Thread a band onto your hook and pull it through the loops on the hook.

3 Your bracelet should now look the same as it did in step 3 of **Making a bracelet by hand**. Continue looping the bands through the previous ones until your bracelet is complete. Finish as in step 5.

Making a bracelet with a loom

SKILL LEVEL ✳

You Will Need

Loom

Assorted bands—
26 per bracelet

Hook

C-clip

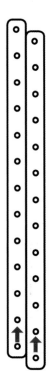

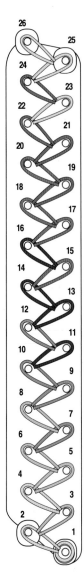

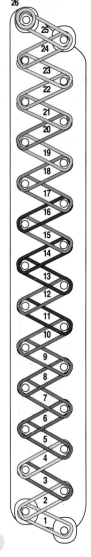

1 Set up your loom in the diagonal format—2 pegs wide x 13 pegs long (see page 10)—with the pointed end facing you. Lay out your bands, following the order shown. Twist a band four times around the last peg to make a cap band.

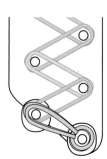

2 Turn the loom around so that the inverted end is facing you. Insert your hook into the bottom peg, pick up the band (not the cap band), and hook it over the opposing peg.

3 Repeat along the whole loom, inserting your hook, picking up the lower band, and hooking it over the opposing peg in the order shown.

4 Attach a C-clip to the cap band and insert your hook into the loops on the top band. Gently pull the bracelet off the loom and insert the loops on your hook into the C-clip.

squared single bracelet

As soon as you start laying out the bands for this bracelet, you will see why it is called a "squared" single! It's a really quick and easy project—ideal for beginners!

SKILL LEVEL ✳

You Will Need

Loom

27 lime-green bands

13 purple bands

Hook

C-clip

LOOM SET-UP

Set up your loom in the diagonal format—3 pegs wide x 26 pegs long (see page 10).

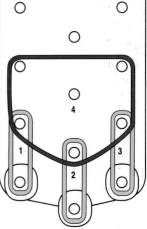

1 With the pointed end of the loom facing you, lay out three lime-green bands vertically on the pegs and then stretch a purple band over the top, following the order shown.

easy-peasy bracelets

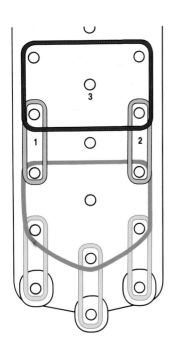

2 Now lay two more lime-green bands vertically from the two top outer pegs and lay a purple band in a square over four pegs.

3 Repeat step 2 all the way up the loom, ending with two vertical lime-green bands.

4 Turn the loom around so that the inverted end is facing you. Insert your hook into peg A, pick up the purple band, and hook it over peg C. Repeat on the right side with the other side of the purple band on peg B, hooking it over peg D. Then hook the lime-green bands on pegs C and D over their opposing pegs. Repeat all the way up the loom.

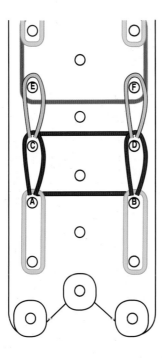

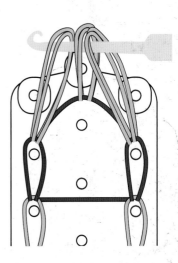

5 Insert your hook into the top three pegs and pick up all the loops, then gently pull the bracelet off the loom, leaving it on the hook.

6 Insert the loops on the hook into a C-clip, then attach the C-clip to the loops at the start of the bracelet to complete.

diamond bracelet

Once you have mastered the single and squared single bracelets, this Diamond Bracelet is the perfect next challenge! Try mixing and matching the arrangement of colors to create different effects and patterns.

SKILL LEVEL ✳

You Will Need

Loom

25 pink bands

24 green bands

Hook

C-clip

LOOM SET-UP

Set up your loom in the diagonal format— 3 pegs wide x 13 pegs long (see page 10).

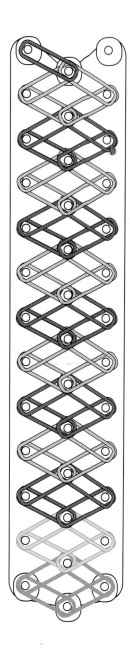

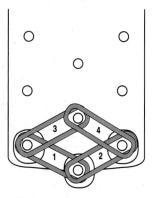

1 With the pointed end of the loom facing you, lay four pink bands in the order shown.

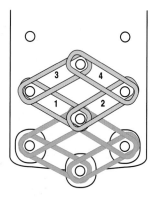

2 Then arrange four green bands as shown.

3 Repeat steps 1 and 2 five times more until your loom is full. Finish with one pink band on the last row.

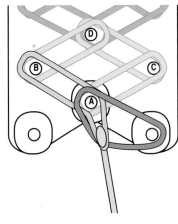

4 Turn your loom around so that the inverted end is facing you. Using the hook, lift the top green band on peg A onto peg B.

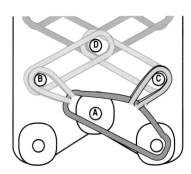

5 Now lift the bottom green band on peg A onto peg C.

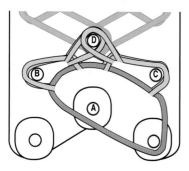

6 Hook the bottom green band on peg B onto peg D, and then the bottom green band on peg C onto peg D. Repeat steps 4 through 6 until you get to the pointed top of the loom.

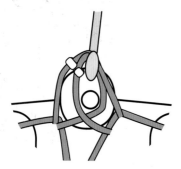

7 Insert your hook into the four loops on the last peg, pull, and attach a C-clip.

8 Gently pull the bracelet off the loom and hook the first pink band onto the C-clip to complete.

further ideas

TO MAKE YOUR BRACELET INTO A NECKLACE OR CHOKER, JOIN TWO LOOMS TOGETHER SO THAT IT IS 3 PEGS WIDE AND 26 PEGS LONG. YOU WILL NEED TWICE AS MANY BANDS AS YOU DID FOR THE BRACELET. FOLLOW THE SAME INSTRUCTIONS AS FOR THE BRACELET. THIS COMBINED WITH THE BRACELET WOULD BE A WONDERFUL GIFT FOR SOMEONE SPECIAL.

triple single cuff

This is an easy but effective stripy cuff that looks so cool! You can make it with solid stripes or, once you've tried that, in a rainbow pattern!

SKILL LEVEL ✳

You Will Need

Loom

13 purple bands

12 turquoise bands

13 pink bands

23 white bands

Hook

C-clip

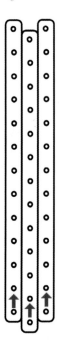

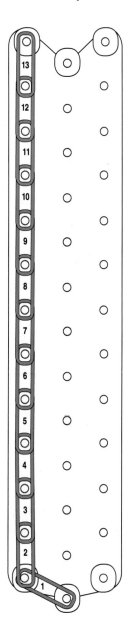

LOOM SET-UP

Set up your loom in the diagonal format—3 pegs wide x 13 pegs long (see page 10).

1 With the pointed end on the loom facing you, lay a purple band from the bottom center peg to the first peg on the left, then lay the remaining purple bands up the left side of the loom.

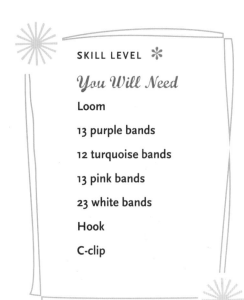

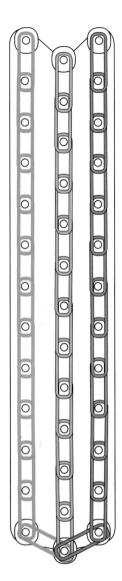

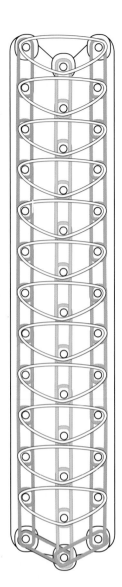

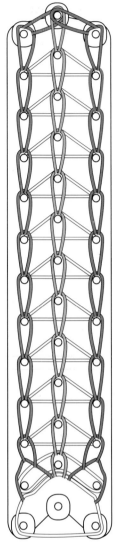

4 Turn the loom around so that the inverted end is facing you. Starting on the left side (with the pink bands), put your hook into the first left peg, pick up the pink band, and loop it over itself. Repeat with all the pinks, then the turquoise center bands, and finally the purple right ones.

2 Lay a row of turquoise bands from the bottom center peg to the top center peg. Then repeat step 1 on the right side of the loom, using the pink bands.

3 Now arrange the white bands in a triangular format, missing the first row of pegs, all the way along the loom.

5 Insert your hook into all the bands on the top peg, stretch, and then feed a white band through all the loops on the hook.

6 Insert your hook into the white band, gently pull the bracelet off the loom. With the loops still on the hook, put the bracelet to one side.

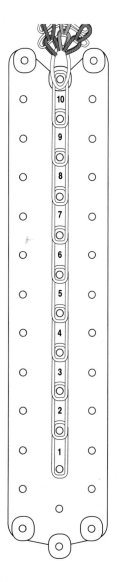

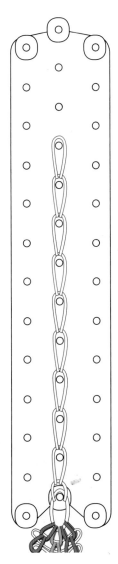

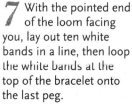

7 With the pointed end of the loom facing you, lay out ten white bands in a line, then loop the white bands at the top of the bracelet onto the last peg.

8 Turn the loom around, so that the inverted end is facing you. Starting on the peg with the bracelet attached, loop the base of each band over the next peg up. Attach a C-clip to the last band on the loom and hook it to the loop at the other end of the bracelet to complete.

further ideas

RAINBOW CUFF

To make the rainbow cuff, you will need two looms joined together lengthwise in the diagonal format (or a homemade loom measuring 26 pegs long by 3 pegs wide).

Lay the bands on the left side as opposite—but instead of using just one color along the whole row, lay 1 x yellow, 1 x orange, 1 x red, 1 x pink, 1 x purple, 1 x dark blue, 1 x light blue, 1 x turquoise, 1 x green. Repeat all the way up the loom.

Repeat the same pattern of loops on the center and right-hand pegs.

Lay out the white bands, as in step 3 opposite.

Turn the loom around so that the inverted end is facing you and complete the bracelet, following steps 4 through 6, opposite. Finish by attaching a C-clip to the top three bands and the first band to make your cuff.

fishtail necklace & bracelet

The fishtail is super-quick to make. You don't even need a loom—just two pegs close together. You could even use the prongs of a fork!

SKILL LEVEL ✳

You Will Need

(for the necklace or bracelet)

Loom, two nails, or a fork

68 gold bands

68 white bands

68 black bands

Hook

Two C-clips

Making the necklace

1 Take a gold band and twist it once into a figure-eight. Place it over two pegs of your loom.

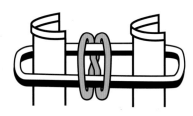

2 Add one black and one white band on top of the twisted gold band; the black and white bands should not be twisted. Insert your hook into the left peg, pick up the gold band, and hook it into the center. Repeat on the right peg with the right side of the gold band.

Making the bracelet

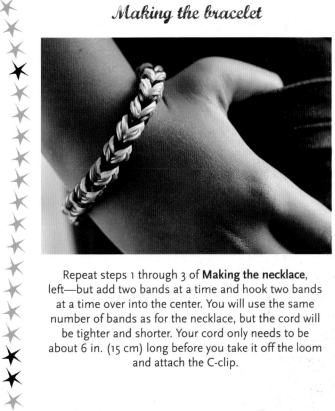

Repeat steps 1 through 3 of **Making the necklace**, left—but add two bands at a time and hook two bands at a time over into the center. You will use the same number of bands as for the necklace, but the cord will be tighter and shorter. Your cord only needs to be about 6 in. (15 cm) long before you take it off the loom and attach the C-clip.

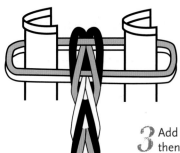

3 Add one gold band, then insert your hook into the left peg, pick up the black band, and hook it into the center. Repeat on the right. Continue adding one band at a time, keeping the color sequence the same throughout and hooking the sides into the center.

4 When your cord is long enough (approx. 12 in./30 cm), insert your hook into the four loops on the two pegs, and pull the necklace off the loom. Thread another band through these loops.

5 Attach the loops on your hook and the loops on the other end of the necklace to a C-clip to complete.

double cross bracelet

The double cross bracelet is a really effective way of showing off your array of band colors! Try splitting them up with a band of white to emphasize their pop of brightness.

SKILL LEVEL ✳

You Will Need

Loom

18 red bands

8 orange bands

8 yellow bands

4 lime-green bands

4 green bands

4 turquoise bands

4 blue bands

4 purple bands

4 pink bands

Hook

C-clip

LOOM SET-UP

Set up your loom in the square format—3 pegs wide x 13 pegs long (see page 10).

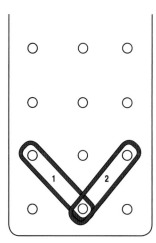

1 Lay two red bands in a V shape.

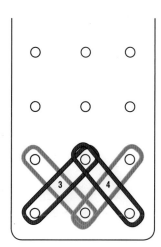

2 Lay two more red bands on top of the first two in an inverted V.

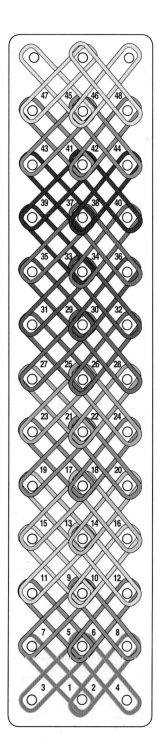

3 Repeat steps 1 and 2 all the way up the loom in the following order: orange, yellow, lime-green, green, turquoise, blue, purple, and pink. Then repeat the red, orange, and yellow once more to fill the loom.

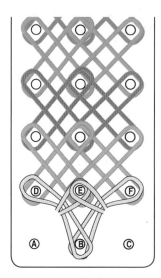

4 Turn the loom around. Insert your hook into peg A, pick up the band, and hook it over peg E. Then repeat on the right side, picking up the band on peg C and hooking it over peg E.

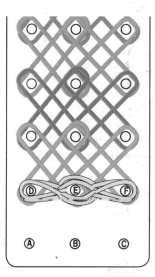

5 Insert your hook into peg B, pick up the top yellow band, and hook it over peg D. Then pick up the remaining band on peg B and hook it over peg F.

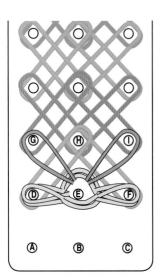

6 Insert your hook into peg E, pick up the top orange band, and hook it over peg G. Go back into peg E, pick up the remaining orange band, and hook it over peg I.

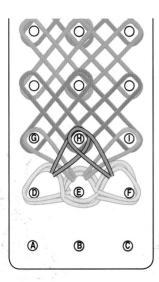

7 Insert your hook into peg D, pick up the orange band, and hook it over peg H. Insert your hook into peg F, pick up the orange band, and hook it over peg H.

8 Repeat steps 6 and 7 all the way up the loom.

further ideas

SET UP YOUR LOOM IN THE SQUARE FORMAT, 3 PEGS WIDE X 26 PEGS LONG. ALTERNATE EACH SET OF 4 COLORED BANDS WITH A SET OF WHITE ONES ALL THE WAY UP THE LOOM. HOOK AS PER THE INSTRUCTIONS AND REMOVE THE BRACELET FROM THE LOOM. JOIN THE ENDS USING A C-CLIP. THERE IS NO NEED TO EXTEND THE BRACELET AS IT WILL BE LONG ENOUGH ALREADY.

9 Insert your hook into the top three pegs, pick up the loops on all those pegs, and gently pull the bracelet off the loom, leaving it on the hook.

10 Extend the bracelet by adding ten more red bands with your hook (see page 15). Attach a C-clip to the loops on the hook and then attach the C-clip to the loops at the start of the bracelet to complete.

totem pole bracelet

This stripy bracelet looks really effective in bold and bright colors. Why not try making it in your school or favorite sports team's colors?

SKILL LEVEL ✳ ✳

You Will Need

Loom

47 yellow bands

22 orange bands

20 turquoise bands

Hook

C-clip

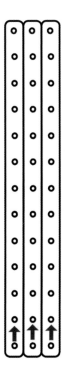

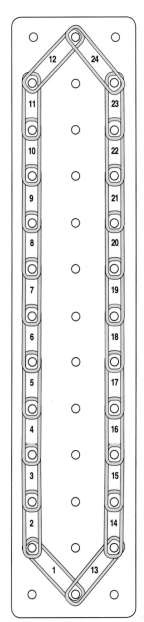

LOOM SET-UP

Set up your loom in the square format—3 pegs wide x 13 pegs long (see page 8).

1 Lay out 24 yellow bands along the two outer sides in the order shown.

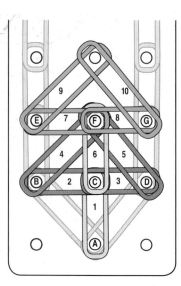

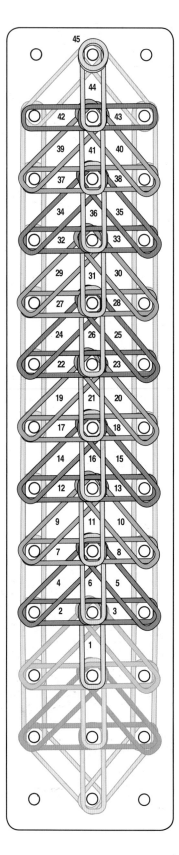

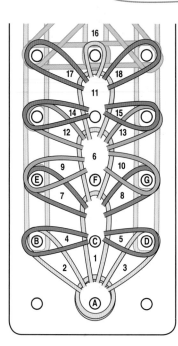

further ideas

THIS WOULD MAKE A
REALLY COOL CHOKER—
JUST MAKE THE LOOM
3 PEGS WIDE x 26 PEGS
LONG AND DOUBLE THE
NUMBER OF BANDS.

2 Lay a yellow band between pegs A and C, then make a triangle with four orange bands in the order specified. Lay another yellow band between pegs C and F, and then make another triangle with four turquoise bands.

3 Repeat step 2 all the way up the loom, finishing with two orange bands and a final yellow band. Twist a yellow band four times around the top peg to make a cap band.

4 Turn the loom around. Insert your hook into the bottom center peg and hook the bands over their opposing pegs in the order shown.

5 Repeat step 4 all the way up the loom.

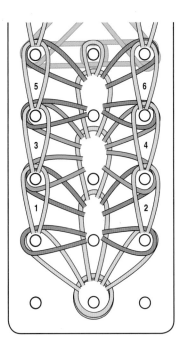

6 Go back to the bottom of the loom and hook the outer yellow bands over their opposing pegs all the way up the loom in the order shown.

7 Insert your hook into the top peg, pick up the all loops, and gently pull the bracelet off the loom.

8 Extend the bracelet by adding ten more yellow bands with your hook (see page 15).

9 Attach a C-clip to the loops on the hook and then attach the C-clip to the loops at the start of the bracelet to complete.

pinstripe cuff

The great thing about this bracelet is that it is reversible! Try it both ways and see which you prefer—the stripy side or the more subtle version.

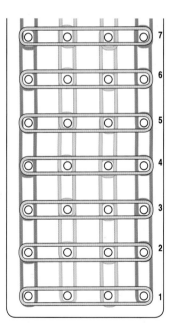

SKILL LEVEL ✳ ✳

You Will Need

Loom

100 red bands

76 turquoise bands

24 lime-green bands

26 silver bands

C-clip

Hook (optional)

LOOM SET-UP

If you're using a store-bought loom, you will need to join eight strips together to make it wide and long enough. Set it up in the square format—4 pegs wide x 26 pegs long (see page 8).

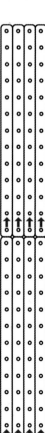

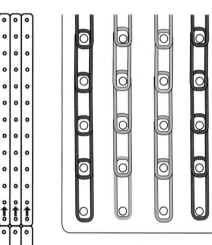

1 Set up the loom. Lay out two red bands on each set of pegs up the left and right sides. Then lay two turquoise bands on the first three rows of the center pegs, followed by two lime-green bands on the central pegs on row 4. Repeat up the length of the loom; the last two rows will have turquoise bands in the center.

2 Now lay one silver band over each row of four horizontal pegs all the way up the loom.

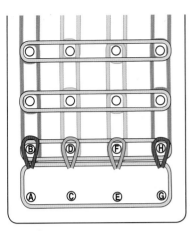

3 Turn the loom around. Insert your hook into peg A and hook the two red bands over peg B. Repeat along the row with pegs C and D, E and F, and G and H.

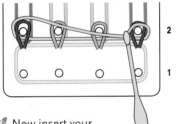

4 Now insert your hook, or use your fingers, to move the top edge of the silver band over row 2 onto row 1.

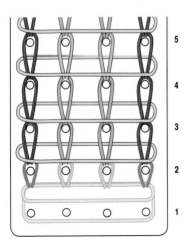

5 Repeat steps 3 and 4 all along the length of the loom.

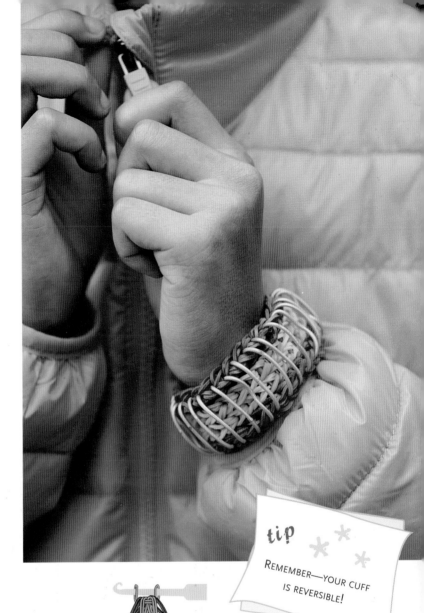

tip ✳ ✳ ✳

REMEMBER—YOUR CUFF IS REVERSIBLE!

6 Attach a C-clip to the bottom silver band and insert your hook into the loops on the top four pegs. Gently pull the cuff off the loom, then thread another band through all 16 loops on the hook.

7 To complete your cuff, attach the loops on your hook to the C-clip on the other end of the cuff.

triple link bracelet
& necklace

This design is really different to all the others in this book, as the round band is the star of the show! Note that the pegs on the loom need to face in alternate directions, so keep this in mind when setting up your loom.

SKILL LEVEL ✳

You Will Need

Loom

26 white bands

24 pink bands

21 turquoise bands

21 lime-green bands

1 white band

Hook

C-clip

LOOM SET-UP

Set up your loom in the square format— 2 pegs wide x 13 pegs long (see page 8) —with the left strip's arrow pointing away from you and the right strip's arrow pointing toward you.

Making the bracelet

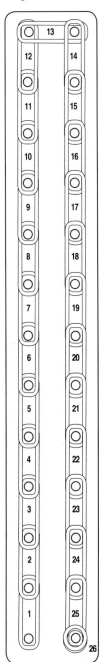

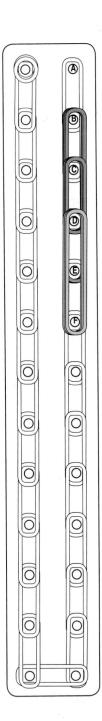

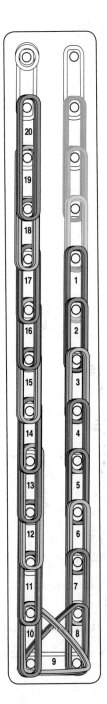

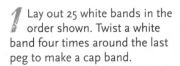 Lay out 25 white bands in the order shown. Twist a white band four times around the last peg to make a cap band.

2 Turn the loom around. Lay three pink bands between pegs B and D, three turquoise bands between pegs C and E, and three lime-green bands between pegs D and F.

3 Repeat step 2 along the whole loom, ending with three pink bands. In the corners, lay the bands over the pegs in a triangular formation.

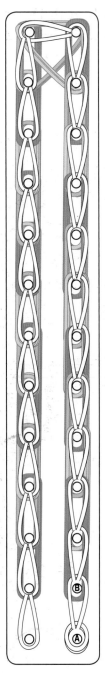

Making the necklace

You Will Need

Loom

65 white bands

63 pink bands

60 turquoise bands

60 blue bands

Hook

C-clip

If you are using a store-bought loom, you will need to join two looms together side by side to make it wide enough. Set up your loom 5 pegs wide x 13 pegs long, with the strips facing in alternate directions. Lay out the white bands as in step 1 of the bracelet, but along all five strips of the loom. Make the necklace, following steps 2 through 6 of the bracelet.

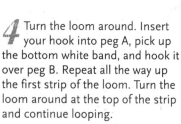

4 Turn the loom around. Insert your hook into peg A, pick up the bottom white band, and hook it over peg B. Repeat all the way up the first strip of the loom. Turn the loom around at the top of the strip and continue looping.

5 Insert your hook into the last peg through all the loops on that peg and gently pull the bracelet off the loom.

6 Insert the loops on the hook into a C-clip and through the cap band at the start of the bracelet to complete.

mohican bracelet

This bracelet looks just like the haircut! This is unlike any of the other projects in the book, as you cross the bands over each other before looping. You'll soon get the hang of it once you start.

SKILL LEVEL *

You Will Need

Loom

26 red bands

44 black bands

Hook

C-clip

LOOM SET-UP

Set up your loom in the diagonal format—3 pegs wide x 13 pegs long (see page 10).

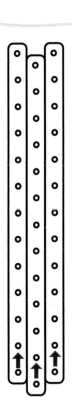

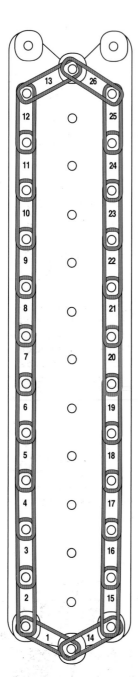

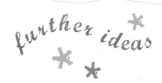

ADD MORE COLOR TO YOUR
MOHICAN BRACELET BY
USING TURQUOISE BANDS
FOR THE EDGES LAID IN
STEP 1, BLACK BANDS FOR
THE CENTRAL ROW, AND RED
BANDS FOR THE DIAGONAL
ONES. CONTRASTING
COLORS LOOK GREAT BUT
YOU WOULD ACHIEVE A
MORE SUBTLE EFFECT IF
YOU USED SIMILAR COLORS
IN THE DESIGN.

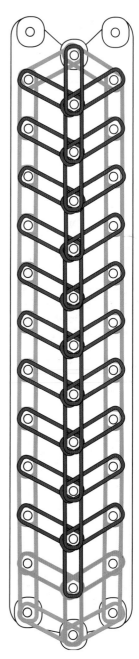

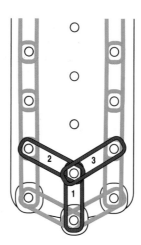

1 With the pointed end of the loom facing you, lay the red bands around the outside pegs of the loom in the order shown.

2 Lay one black band from the bottom center peg to the peg above, a diagonal black band from the second center peg to the left peg, and another diagonal black band from the second center peg to the right peg.

3 Repeat step 2 all the way up the loom.

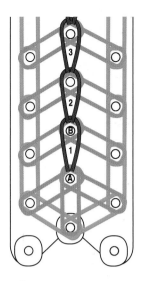

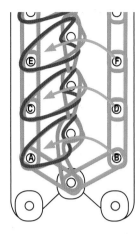

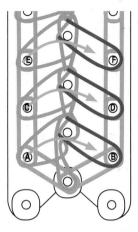

4 Turn the loom around so that the inverted end is facing you. Insert your hook into peg A, pick up the bottom band, and hook it over peg B. Repeat this looping all the way up the loom.

5 Go back to the bottom of the loom, pick up the black band on peg B, and hook it over peg A. Repeat this looping all the way up the loom.

6 Go back to the bottom of the loom, insert your hook into peg A, pick up the bottom band, and hook it over peg B. You have now twisted the bands over each other. Repeat all the way up the loom.

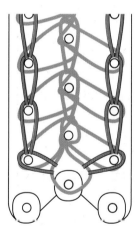

8 Insert your hook into the top center peg through all the loops and pull the bracelet gently off the loom, leaving it on the hook. Using your hook (see page 15), add ten more black bands to the bracelet to make it long enough to fit around your wrist.

9 Insert the loops on the hook into a C-clip, then attach the C-clip to the loops at the start of the bracelet to complete.

7 Go back to the bottom of the loom. Starting in the center peg, pick up the top red band and hook it over its opposing peg. Repeat, working all the way up the left side of the loom and then all the way up the right side.

This is a quick-and-easy little project. I think it works better with double white bands, but you could make it with single bands if you prefer.

confetti bracelet

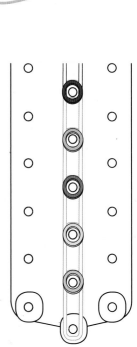

You Will Need

Loom

52 white bands

5 fluorescent blue bands

5 fluorescent yellow bands

5 fluorescent orange bands

5 fluorescent green bands

5 fluorescent purple bands

Hook

C-clip

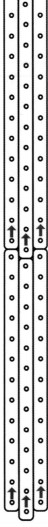

LOOM SET-UP

If you are using a store-bought loom, you will need to join two looms together lengthwise to make it long enough. Set up your loom in the diagonal format— 3 pegs wide x 26 pegs long (see page 10).

1 With the pointed end of the loom facing you, lay two white bands between each pair of pegs along the center row of the loom.

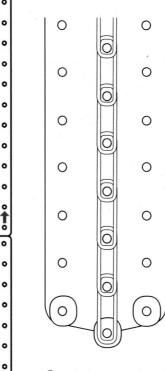

2 Place a cap band on each peg except the first one, by twisting a band four times around the peg in the following color sequence: blue, yellow, orange, green, and purple. Repeat this all the way up the loom.

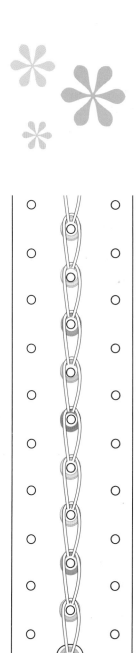

3 Turn the loom around so that the inverted end is facing you. Insert your hook into the first peg. Pick up the white bands on the peg and hook them over the next peg up. Repeat this all the way up the loom.

4 Insert your hook into the top peg and through all the loops on that peg. Pull the bracelet gently off the loom, leaving it on the hook.

5 Insert the loops on the hook into a C-clip, then slip the C-clip through the cap band at the start of the bracelet to complete.

dragon-scale bracelet

This bracelet uses a different technique of looping compared to other projects in this book. Try it out and make yourself a cool dragon-scale effect cuff.

SKILL LEVEL ✳✳

You Will Need

Loom

48 yellow bands

30 turquoise bands

Hook

3 C-clips

LOOM SET-UP

Your loom needs to be at least 6 pegs long and turned so that it runs horizontally. You will only use one strip of the loom, but it is best to use a loom that is 3 pegs wide to stop it from falling over when you are working.

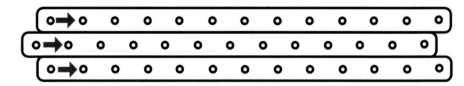

1 Twist a yellow band into a figure-eight and lay it between pegs A and B. Repeat with two more yellow bands between pegs C and D, and pegs E and F.

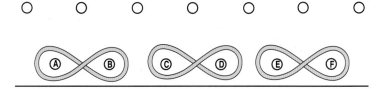

2 Twist a turquoise band into a figure-eight and place it between pegs B and C. Repeat with another turquoise band between pegs D and E.

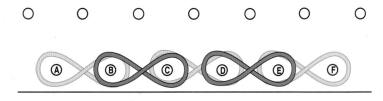

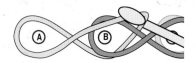 

3 Starting on peg B, pick up the bottom yellow band with your hook and hook it forward over peg B. If the yellow band isn't twisted after you've done this, lift it off peg A: it will automatically twist and then you can replace it on peg A.

4 Repeat on pegs C, D, and E.

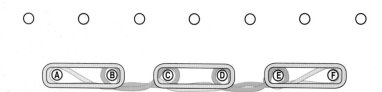

5 Place untwisted yellow bands over pegs A and B, pegs C and D, and pegs E and F.

6 Using the same hooking forward technique as in step 3, pick up the bottom yellow band on peg A and hook it over the front of the peg. Repeat on pegs B to E, picking up the bottom turquoise band and hooking it forward over the peg. On peg F, pick up the bottom yellow band, and hook it over peg F.

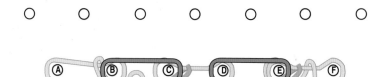

7 Place untwisted turquoise bands over pegs B and C, and pegs D and E.

8 Using the same hooking forward technique as in step 3, pick up the bottom yellow band on peg B and hook it over the front of the peg. Repeat on pegs C, D, and E.

9 Repeat steps 5 through 8 until you have 15 rows of yellow bands and 15 rows of turquoise bands.

10 Insert your hook into the loops on pegs F and E, pull them off the loom, and thread another yellow band through the loops on the hook.

MAKE A CHUNKIER VERSION
OF THE CUFF BY ADDING
TWO BANDS INSTEAD OF
ONE EACH TIME AND
PICKING UP THE TWO
BOTTOM BANDS TO HOOK
FORWARD. YOU CAN ALSO
EXPERIMENT WITH COLOR
VARIATIONS AND PATTERNS
ONCE YOU HAVE MASTERED
THE TECHNIQUE!

11 Thread one end through the other and pull tight to secure.

12 Repeat with the loops on pegs D and C, and B and A.

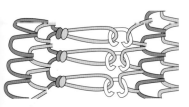

13 Attach a C-clip to each securing loop and to the bands at the start of the bracelet to complete.

chapter 2

craftier bracelets

butterfly necklace

This pretty butterfly necklace is just so easy to make!
Try using only one loom to make a matching bracelet.

SKILL LEVEL ✳

You Will Need

Loom

49 blue bands

36 turquoise bands

24 lime-green bands

24 white bands

Hook

C-clip

LOOM SET-UP

If you're using a store-bought loom, you will need to join two together to make it long enough. Set up the loom in the diagonal format—3 pegs wide x 26 pegs long (see page 10).

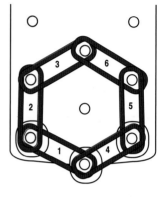

1 With the pointed end of the loom facing you, loop six blue bands over the pegs in a hexagonal pattern, following the order shown.

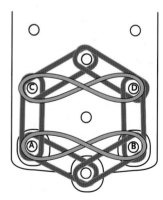

2 Take two lime-green bands, twist once into a figure-eight, and hook over pegs A and B. Repeat with another two lime-green bands on pegs C and D.

3 Repeat steps 1 and 2 with the turquoise and white bands.

4 Repeat steps 1 through 3 all the way up the loom. Add a cap band to the top center peg by twisting a blue band around it 4 times.

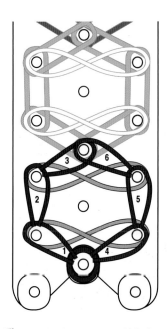

5 Turn the loom around so that the inverted end is facing you. Insert your hook into the bottom center peg. Take the top blue band (excluding the cap band) and hook it over the opposing peg. Repeat with all the bands in the hexagon in the order specified.

6 Repeat step 5 all the way up the loom.

butterfly necklace

7 Insert your hook into the top central peg through all the loops on the peg and gently pull the necklace off the loom.

8 Using your hook, thread 12 extra blue bands onto the necklace to make it long enough to go around your neck (see page 15); you may need to reduce or increase the number of extra bands depending on the size of your neck!

9 Add a C-clip through the loops on the hook and through the cap band loops at the other end of the necklace to complete.

starburst bracelet

This is one of the most popular rubber-band bracelets around—ideal for both girls and boys.

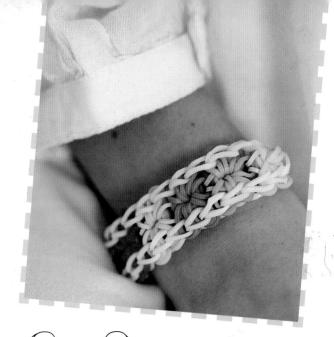

SKILL LEVEL ✳ ✳

You Will Need

Loom

36 white bands

7 yellow bands

7 light blue bands

7 orange bands

7 green bands

7 red bands

8 dark blue bands

Hook

C-clip

LOOM SET-UP

Set up the loom in a diagonal format—3 pegs wide x 13 pegs long (see page 10).

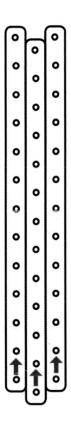

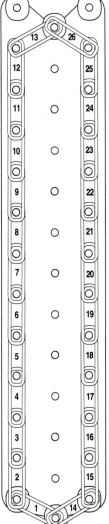

1 With the pointed end of the loom facing you, lay one white band on each set of pegs in the order shown.

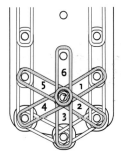

2 Lay one yellow band on each set of pegs in the order shown to make a star shape, then add a cap band to the center peg of the star by twisting a yellow band around it four times.

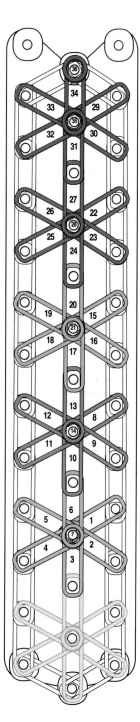

3 Repeat step 2 with the light blue, orange, green, red, and dark blue bands. Add a dark blue cap band to the top peg.

4 Turn the loom around so that the inverted end is facing you. Insert your hook into the bottom center peg, pick up the top dark blue band under the cap band, and hook it over the opposing peg (the center peg of the hexagon). Repeat with all the bands in the star, following the order shown.

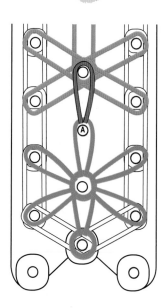

5 For the second star, insert your hook into the bottom peg of the star (peg A), pick up the red band and hook it over the center peg.

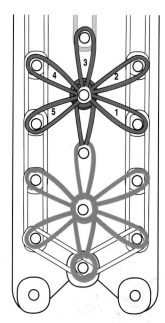

6 Continue hooking the rest of the star by inserting your hook into the central peg and hooking the bands onto their opposing pegs in the order shown. Repeat steps 5 and 6 on all the remaining stars.

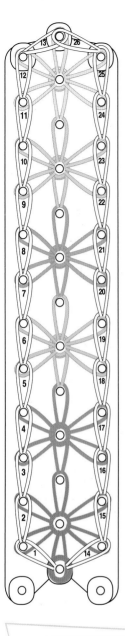

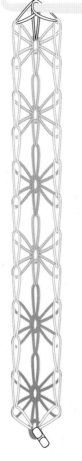

7 Now go back to the bottom of the loom and hook all the white bands onto their opposing pegs in the order specified.

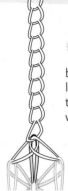

8 Add a C-clip to the cap band at the bottom of the loom and then insert your hook into the loops at the top of the loom. Gently pull the bracelet off the loom. With the loops still on the hook, put the bracelet to one side.

9 Using your hook, add 10 more white bands to extend the length of the bracelet so that it fits around your wrist (see page 15).

10 Hook the loops on your hook onto the C-clip at the other end of the bracelet to complete.

further ideas
✳ ✳ ✳

TRY USING BLACK AS YOUR OUTER COLOR FOR A STRIKING LOOK—IT REALLY MAKES THE COLORS POP OUT!

twisted liberty bracelet

The twisted effect of this bracelet looks more complicated to create than it is. Try making it in your friend's favorite colors for a great gift.

SKILL LEVEL ✳✳

You Will Need

Loom

30 purple bands

25 pink bands

25 blue bands

Hook

C-clip

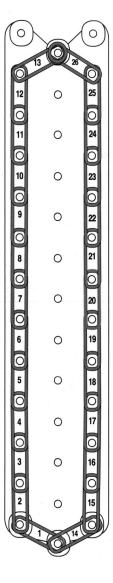

1 With the pointed end of the loom facing you, lay out the purple bands around the edge of the loom in the order shown. Add a cap band around the top central peg by twisting one purple band around it four times.

LOOM SET-UP

Set up your loom in a diagonal format—3 pegs wide x 13 pegs long (see page 10).

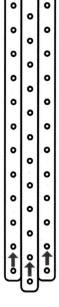

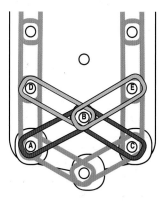

2 Lay one pink band between peg A and peg B and another between peg B and peg C. Then lay a blue band between peg D and peg B and another between peg B and peg E.

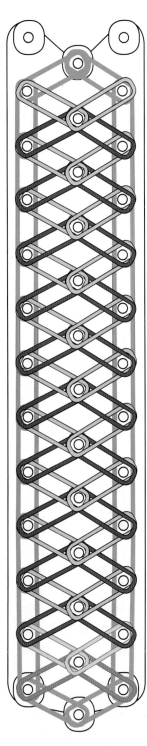

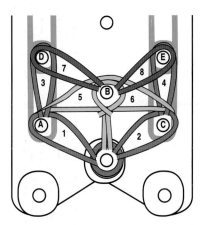

3 Repeat step 2 all the way up the loom.

4 Turn the loom around so that the inverted end is facing you and insert your hook into the bottom center peg. Pick up the purple band underneath the cap band and hook it over the opposing peg (move 1). Repeat with the other band on that central peg (move 2). Then hook the bottom loop of the first purple side band on each side over its top peg (moves 3 and 4).

Now hook the blue bands over their opposing central pegs: insert your hook into peg A, pick up the blue band and hook it over peg B (move 5).

Repeat with the blue band on the other side between pegs C and B (move 6).

Finally, insert your hook into peg B, pick up the pink band, and hook it over peg D (move 7). Repeat with the pink band on the other side between pegs B and E (move 8).

5 Continue up the loom, hooking the bands in the same order specified in step 4 (excluding moves 1 and 2). Hook the top two purple bands over the central top peg.

6 Insert your hook into the loops on the top central pegs and pull the bracelet gently off the loom. With the loops still on the hook, put the bracelet to one side.

7 With the pointed end of the loom facing you, lay out nine more bands on the loom, alternating the colors as shown. Then loop the bracelet onto the last peg with a band.

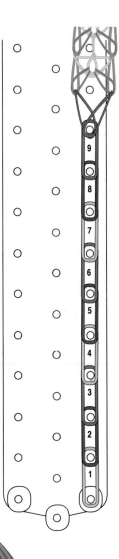

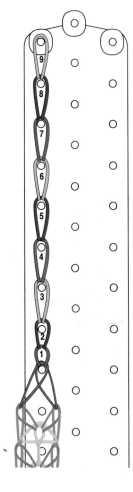

8 Turn the loom around so that the inverted end is facing you. Insert your hook into the peg with the bracelet attached and loop the base of each band over the next peg up in the order shown.

9 Insert your hook into the loops on the last peg and pull off the loom. Attach a C-clip to the bands and to the cap band at the other end of the bracelet to complete.

arrow bracelet

This arrow bracelet is striking! Although it looks really effective, it can be tricky—the key is to make sure you lay the bands in step 4 the right way. This bracelet is reversible—choose which side you prefer!

SKILL LEVEL ✳ ✳ ✳

You Will Need

Loom

26 fluorescent green bands

23 fluorescent yellow bands

36 fluorescent pink bands

Hook

C-clip

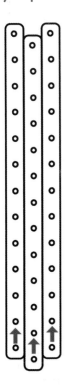

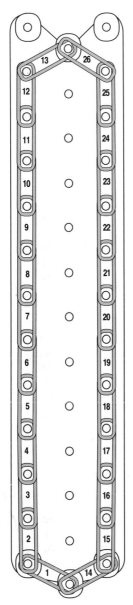

LOOM SET-UP

Set up your loom in the diagonal format—3 pegs wide x 13 pegs long (see page 10).

1 With the pointed end of the loom facing you, lay out the green bands in the order shown.

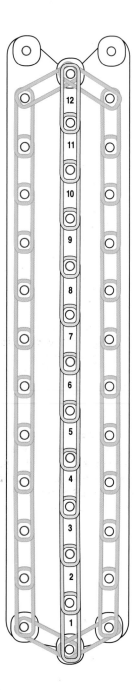

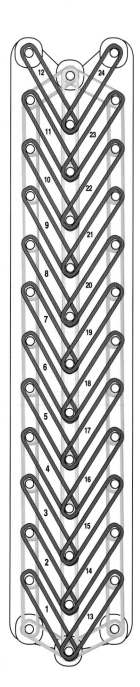

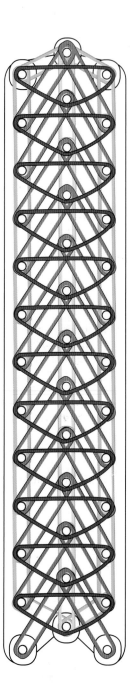

2 Lay the yellow bands along the center pegs in the order shown.

3 Lay pink bands diagonally from the center peg to the outer pegs in the order shown. Note these are laid one peg up from where the normal diagonal would be. Start on the left side of the loom and then work on the right.

4 Turn the loom around so that the inverted end is facing you. Lay pink bands in a triangular formation in exactly the way shown. This is very important as your bracelet will not look the same if you place them upside down!

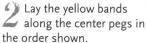

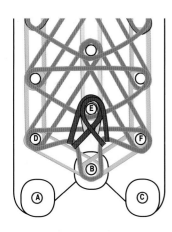
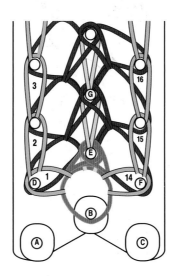
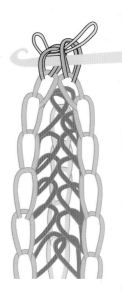

5 Insert your hook into peg B, pick up the yellow band, and hook it over peg E. Then insert your hook into peg A, pick up the pink band, and hook it over peg E. Finally, insert your hook into peg C, pick up the pink band, and hook it over peg E.

6 Repeat step 5 all the way up the loom.

7 Now go back to the bottom of the loom. Insert your hook into peg B, pick up the top green band, and hook it over peg D. Go into peg D, pick up the green band, and hook it over peg G. Repeat all up the side of the loom and then on the other side.

8 Insert your hook into the top peg and thread a yellow band through all the loops on the peg. Gently pull the bracelet off the loom.

9 Using your hook (see page 15), add ten more yellow bands to the bracelet and then hook all the loops onto a C-clip. Attach to the other end of the bracelet to complete.

further ideas

TRY MIXING UP YOUR COLORS TO CREATE DIFFERENT EFFECTS—BY ALTERNATING THE COLORS USED IN STEP 3, YOU CAN MAKE THE OTHER BRACELET SHOWN.

twisted wave bracelet

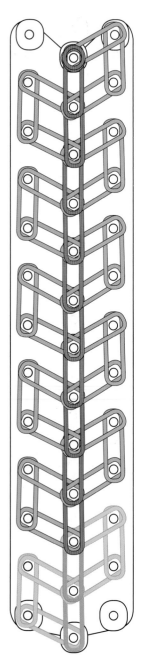

This is my favorite project in the book—it's simple but so effective. Try playing around with the number of bands you lay down in steps 1 and 2 to make thinner or thicker bracelets.

SKILL LEVEL ✳ ✳

You Will Need

Loom

20 pink bands

36 turquoise bands

Hook

C-clip

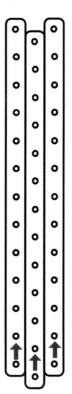

LOOM SET-UP

Set up your loom in the diagonal format—3 pegs wide x 13 pegs long (see page 10).

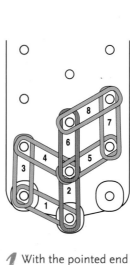

1 With the pointed end of the loom facing you, lay out the bands in the order shown.

2 Repeat step 1 all the way up the loom. Twist a pink band four times around the top center peg to make a cap band.

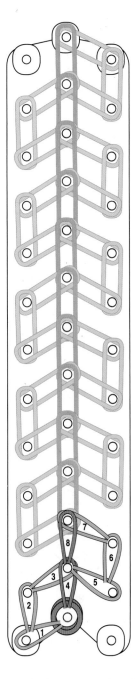

3 Turn the loom around so that the inverted end is facing you. Insert your hook into the bottom center peg, pick up the top turquoise band, and hook it over its opposing peg. Continue hooking the bands over their opposing pegs in the order shown.

4 Repeat step 3 all the way up the loom.

5 Insert your hook into the top peg and through all the loops on that peg, and gently pull the bracelet off the loom, leaving it on the hook.

6 Using your hook (see page 15), add seven more turquoise bands to the bracelet to make it long enough to fit around your wrist.

7 Insert the loops on the hook into a C-clip and through the cap band at the start of the bracelet sto complete.

kaleidoscope bracelet

This bracelet looks fabulous, but will take a bit of time and practice. Try mixing and matching the colors for an even more psychedelic effect!

SKILL LEVEL ✳ ✳ ✳

You Will Need

Loom

36 silver bands

18 dark blue bands

36 turquoise bands

18 white bands

21 purple bands

Hook

C-clip

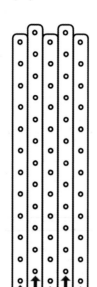

LOOM SET-UP

If you're using a store-bought loom, you will need to join two looms together to make it wide enough. Set it up in the diagonal format—5 pegs wide x 13 pegs long (see page 10).

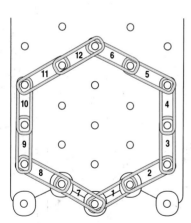

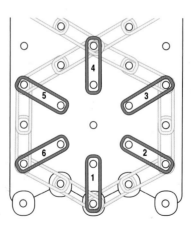

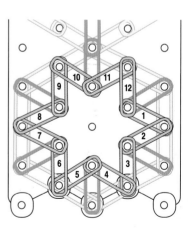

1 With the center point of the loom facing you, loop 12 silver bands over the pegs in a hexagonal pattern, following the order shown. Repeat twice more to the end of the loom.

2 Add six blue bands going into the center of the first hexagon. Repeat on the other two hexagons.

3 Add 12 turquoise bands in a star formation, following the order shown. Repeat on the other two hexagons.

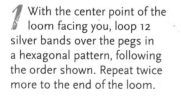

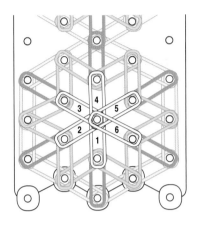

4 Then put six white bands in the center of each hexagon, following the order shown.

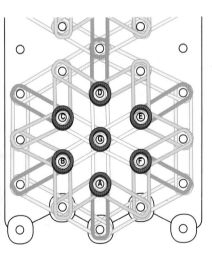

5 Finally, twist purple bands three times around pegs A through G to create cap bands.

6 Turn the loom around so that the inverted end is facing you. Insert the hook into the center peg of the first hexagon, pick up the top white band, and hook it over peg C. Repeat, hooking the bands in a counterclockwise direction, in the order specified. Repeat with the other two hexagons.

7 Insert the hook into peg B, take the top turquoise band, and hook it over peg H. Repeat, going into peg A and hooking the top band over peg H. Continue all the way around in a counterclockwise direction, hooking the base of each turquoise band over the top peg that it's attached to, so that both ends of the band are on the same peg, making sure you hook them in the order shown. Then go around again, hooking the base of each dark blue band over its top peg. Repeat with the other two hexagons.

Twist a silver band three times around the bottom center peg to create a cap band. Working counterclockwise from peg G, hook the base of each silver band over its top peg in the order shown. Repeat with the other two hexagons.

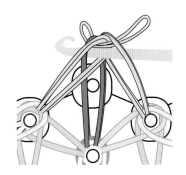

Insert your hook into all the loops on the top peg, stretch, and insert a silver band. Then insert your hook into the silver band and gently pull the bracelet off the loom. With the loops still on the hook, put the bracelet to one side.

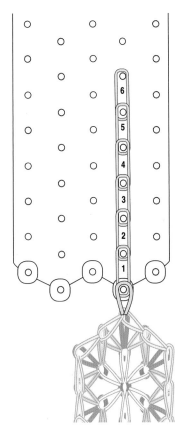

10 With the inverted end of the loom facing you, lay out six silver bands in a line in the order shown, then loop the bracelet onto the last peg facing you.

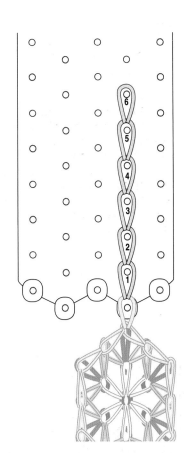

11 With the inverted end of the loom still facing you and starting on the peg with the bracelet attached, loop the base of each silver band over the next peg up in the order shown. Attach a C-clip to the last bands on the loom, and hook the C-clip to the band at the other end of the bracelet to complete.

double braid bracelet

Try using metallic bands for this bracelet, as they look really sophisticated and like real gold jewelry! Note that the bands in this pattern are very taut, so they can snap very easily—so be careful.

SKILL LEVEL ✳ ✳ ✳

You Will Need

Loom

52 gold bands

24 red bands

24 green bands

Hook

C-clip

LOOM SET-UP

If you are using a store-bought loom, you will need to join two looms together lengthwise to make it long enough. Set up your loom in the diagonal format—2 pegs wide x 26 pegs long (see page 10).

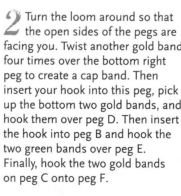

1 With the arrows on the loom pointing away from you, loop two gold bands from peg A to peg D, two red bands from peg B to peg E, two more gold bands from peg C to peg F, and two green bands from peg D to peg G. Repeat this step 11 times more, all the way up the loom.

2 Turn the loom around so that the open sides of the pegs are facing you. Twist another gold band four times over the bottom right peg to create a cap band. Then insert your hook into this peg, pick up the bottom two gold bands, and hook them over peg D. Then insert the hook into peg B and hook the two green bands over peg E. Finally, hook the two gold bands on peg C onto peg F.

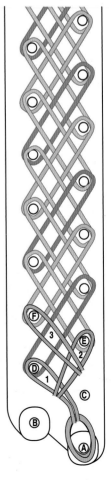

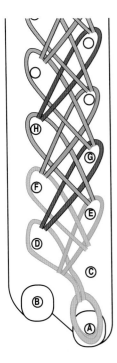

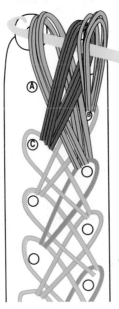

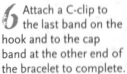

3 Go back into peg D and hook the two bottom red bands over peg G, then go into peg E and hook the two bottom gold bands over peg H. Repeat these two moves all the way up the loom.

4 Insert the hook through the four loops on each of pegs A, B, and C, so that there are 12 loops on your hook, then gently pull the bracelet off the loom.

5 Take another gold band and pull it through the loops on your hook.

6 Attach a C-clip to the last band on the hook and to the cap band at the other end of the bracelet to complete.

Sssssss..... This design really reminds me of a snakeskin. Rather than just making a bracelet, try making a choker with your bands so that it can be seen by everyone.

snake choker

SKILL LEVEL ✳ ✳ ✳

You Will Need

Loom

77 orange bands

25 lime-green bands

51 turquoise bands

Hook

C-clip

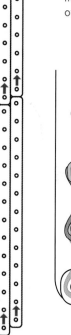

LOOM SET-UP

You will need to join two looms together lengthwise to make it long enough. Set up your loom in the diagonal format—3 pegs wide x 26 pegs long (see page 10).

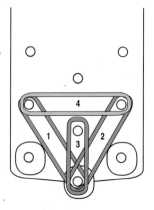

1 With the pointed end of the loom facing you, lay out three orange bands in the order shown. Place a lime-green band horizontally over the two top pegs.

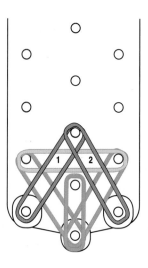

2 Now lay two turquoise bands diagonally, as shown.

3 Repeat steps 1 and 2 up the whole loom, leaving out the third orange band on step 1; the sequence to follow is two diagonal orange bands, one horizontal lime-green band, two diagonal turquoise bands.

4 Twist a turquoise band four times around the top center peg to make a cap band.

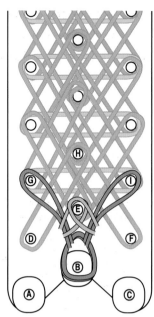

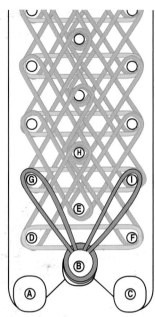

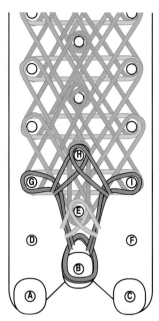

5 Turn the loom around so that the inverted end is facing you. Insert your hook into peg B, pick up the top turquoise band below the cap band, and hook it over peg G. Then go back into peg B, pick up the bottom turquoise band, and hook it over peg I.

6 Now insert your hook into peg D, pick up the lime-green band, and hook it over peg E. Repeat on the other side with the green band on peg F, hooking it over peg E.

7 Now insert your hook into peg D, pick up the orange band, and hook it over peg H. Insert your hook into peg F, pick up the orange band and hook it over peg H.

8 Repeat steps 5 through 7 all the way up the loom.

9 Insert your hook through all the loops on the top three pegs. Gently pull off the loom and thread an orange band through the loops on the hook.

10 Using your hook (see page 15), add 25 more orange bands to make the choker long enough to fit around your neck.

11 Insert the loops on the hook into a C-clip, then attach the C-clip to the loops at the start of the choker to complete.

This is quite a technical design and the loom set-up is very different to the ones used in all the other projects, so read through all the instructions very carefully before you start. It's well worth the effort, though!

herringbone bracelet

SKILL LEVEL ✳ ✳ ✳

You Will Need

Loom

82 white bands

60 blue bands

60 red bands

Hook

C-clip

LOOM SET-UP

If you're using a store-bought loom, you will need to join two looms together side by side to make it wide enough. Set up your loom in an inverted V-format —5 pegs wide x 13 pegs long (see page 10).

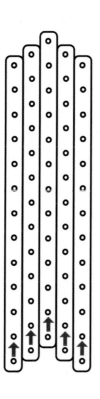

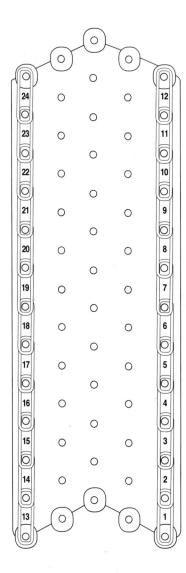

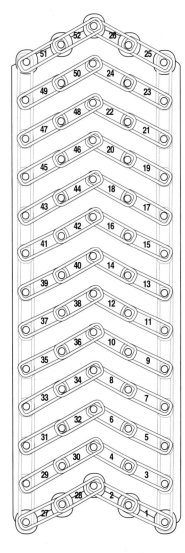

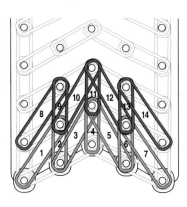

3 Lay out a row of blue bands and a row of red bands in the order specified. Repeat all the way up the loom.

1 Lay out 24 white bands along the sides of the loom, in the order shown.

2 Now lay out the remaining white bands diagonally in the order shown—first from the right-hand side pegs to the center pegs and then from the left-hand side pegs to the center pegs.

4 On the three center pegs of each row except the bottom row, twist a band around the peg four times to make a cap band.

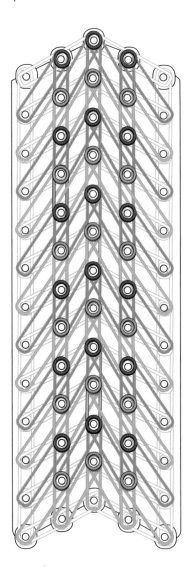

5 Turn the loom around. Insert your hook into peg B, pick up the top red band underneath the cap band, and hook it over peg F, then pick up the remaining red band on peg B and hook it over peg G. Repeat along the row, hooking the bands over their opposing pegs in the order shown.

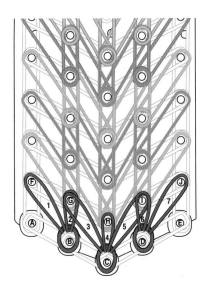

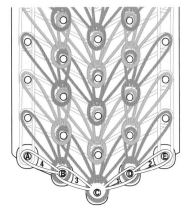

6 Repeat step 5 all the way up the loom.

7 Go back to the bottom of the loom. Insert your hook into peg C, pick up the top white band, and hook it over peg D, then pick up the bottom white band on peg D and hook it over peg E. Repeat on the left bands, working from the center outward.

8 Repeat step 7 up the whole loom.

9 Go back to the bottom of the loom and hook the side white bands over their opposing pegs all the way up.

10 Insert your hook into the top right peg, pick up all the loops on that peg, then repeat on the top left peg. Gently pull the bracelet off the loom, leaving the bracelet on the hook.

11 Using your hook (see page 15), add six more white bands to the bracelet to make it long enough to fit around your wrist.

12 Insert the loops on the hook into a C-clip, then attach the C-clip to the loops at the start of the bracelet to complete.

herringbone bracelet   81

heart bracelet

Show your loved ones you care with this heart bracelet—a great Valentine or Mother's Day gift.

SKILL LEVEL ✳ ✳ ✳

You Will Need

Loom

49 white bands

6 silver bands

15 pink bands

Hook

C-clip

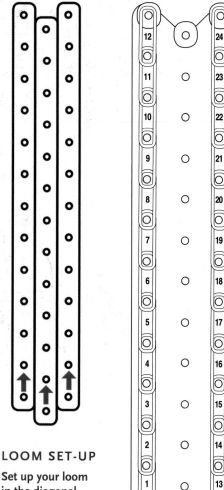

1 With the pointed end of the loom facing you, lay out 24 white bands along the two outer sides in the order shown.

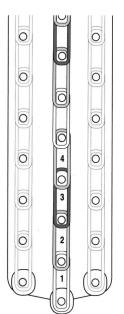

2 Working upward from the bottom of the loom, lay out one white, one silver, one pink, and one silver band along the central row. Fill the rest of this row in the following sequence: white, silver, pink, silver, white, silver, pink, silver.

LOOM SET-UP

Set up your loom in the diagonal format—3 pegs wide x 13 pegs long (see page 10).

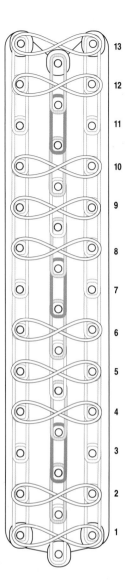

_3_ Twist a white band once into a figure-eight and lay it horizontally between the outer pegs on rows 1, 2, 4, 5, 6, 8, 9, 10, 12, and 13.

_4_ On each peg with a pink band, twist another pink band four times around the peg to make a cap band.

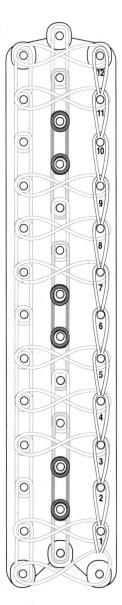

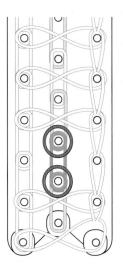

6 Place a pink band over each peg on which you put a pink cap band in step 4.

8 Twist a white band three times around your hook and pull another white band through it.

5 Turn your loom around so that the inverted end is facing you. Insert your hook into the bottom right peg. Pick up the bottom white band and hook it over the opposing peg. Repeat all the way up the right-hand side of the loom.

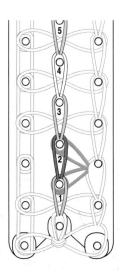

7 Insert your hook into the white band to the right of the first pink band. Pick up the pink band on peg A, pull it through the white band, and hook it over peg B. Repeat with the band on peg B, pulling it though the white band and onto peg A. Repeat on the other pink bands on the loom.

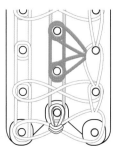

9 Place one end of this band over the bottom center peg, underneath the horizontal band, and then hook the other end of the band on the top of the same peg, over the horizontal band.

10 Hook the central row of bands over their opposing pegs above, all the way up the loom.

x

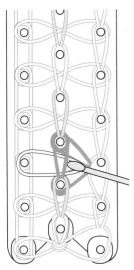

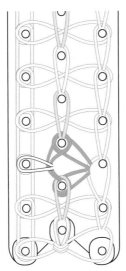

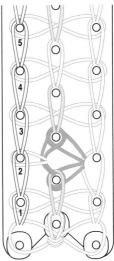

11 Place a white band on the peg to the left of the first pink band. Insert your hook into the small triangle formed in the pink band, and pick up the white band with your hook.

12 Pull the white band through the triangle and back onto the same peg. Repeat steps 11 and 12 on the other two pink bands.

13 Insert your hook into the bottom left peg. Pick up the bottom white band and hook it over the opposing peg. Repeat all the way up the left-hand side of the loom.

14 Put your hook into the top three pegs, through all eight loops, and gently pull the bracelet off the loom, leaving it on the hook. Using your hook (see page 15), add ten more white bands to the bracelet to make it long enough to fit around your wrist.

15 Insert the loops on the hook into a C-clip and attach the C-clip to the loops at the start of the bracelet to complete.

The pink bands on this bracelet form a cage in which all the other bands are trapped. It is a really fun and quirky design—one of my favorites!

zippy chain bracelet

SKILL LEVEL ✳ ✳ ✳

You Will Need

Loom

63 yellow bands

24 turquoise bands

44 pink bands

Hook

C-clip

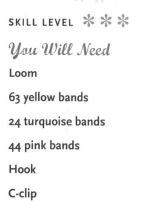

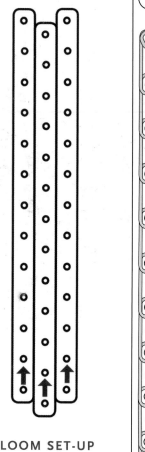

LOOM SET-UP

Set up your loom in the diagonal format—3 pegs wide x 13 pegs long (see page 10).

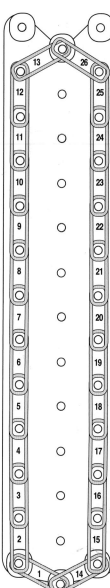

1 With the pointed end of the loom facing you, lay out 26 pairs of yellow bands in the order shown.

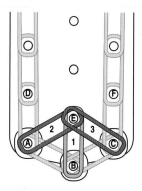

2 Lay two turquoise bands between pegs B and E, two pink bands between pegs A and E, and another two pink bands between pegs E and C.

3 Repeat step 2 all the way up the loom, ending with a turquoise band. Twist a yellow band four times around the top center peg to make a cap band.

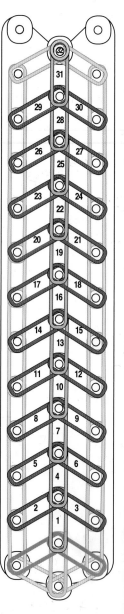

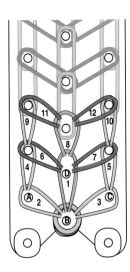

4 Turn the loom around so that the inverted end is facing you. Insert your hook into peg B, pick up the top two turquoise bands underneath the cap band, and hook them over peg D. Go back into peg B, pick up the top two yellow bands, and hook them over peg A. Go back into peg B, pick up the remaining two yellow bands, and hook them over peg C. Continue looping in the order shown.

5 Repeat step 4 all the way up the loom.

6 Insert your hook into the top center peg through all the loops on that peg and gently pull the bracelet off the loom, leaving it on the hook.

7 Using your hook (see page 15), add ten more yellow bands to the bracelet to make it long enough to fit around your wrist.

8 Insert the loops on the hook into a C-clip and then attach the C-clip to the loops at the start of the bracelet to complete.

ladybug & bee bracelets

"Bee" cool with these bug bracelets! With two designs to try, you'll "bee" busy for ages!

Bee bracelet

SKILL LEVEL ✳ ✳ ✳

You Will Need

Loom

9 green bands

24 red bands

6 pink bands

6 black bands

25 yellow bands

6 white bands

Hook

C-clip

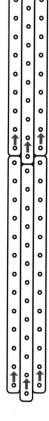

LOOM SET-UP

If you're using a store-bought loom, you will need to join two looms together lengthwise to make a loom long enough for each of these projects. Set it up in the diagonal format—3 pegs wide x 26 pegs long (see page 10).

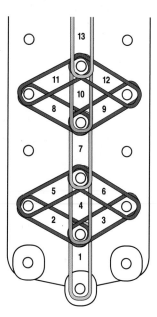

1 With the pointed end of the loom facing you, lay out the green, red, and pink bands in the order shown to make your first flower sequence.

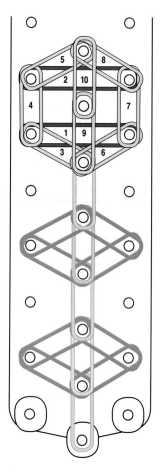

2 To make the bee, lay out two black bands horizontally, then add a hexagon of yellow bands, and finally two yellow bands vertically down the center of your hexagon in the order shown.

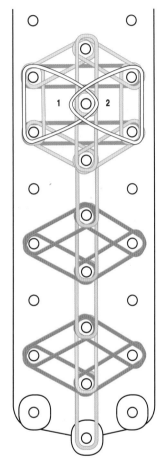

3 Add the wings of the bee by laying two white bands in triangle shapes.

4 Repeat steps 1 through 3 twice, then twist a yellow band four times around the top central peg to make a cap band.

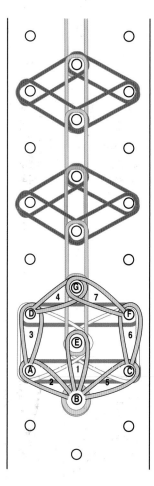
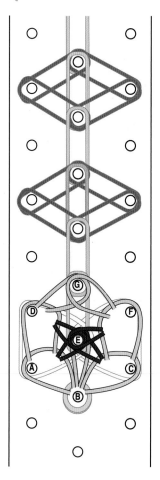
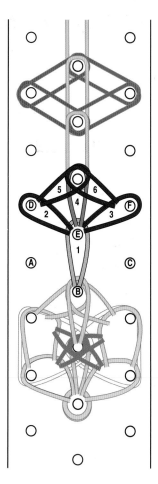

5 Turn the loom around so that the inverted end is facing you. Insert your hook into peg B, pick up the first yellow band underneath the cap band, and hook it over peg E. Then insert your hook back into peg B, pick up the next yellow band down, and hook it over peg A. Continue looping in the order shown.

6 Now hook the black bands: insert your hook into peg A, pick up the black band, and hook it over peg E. Repeat with the black bands on pegs C, D, and F so that they are all on peg E.

7 To complete the bee, insert your hook into peg E, pick up the yellow band, and hook it over peg G.

8 To create the flowers, insert your hook into peg B, pick up the green band, and hook it over peg E. Go into peg E, pick up the top red band, and hook it over peg D, then go back into E, pick up the next red band, and hook it over peg F. Continue hooking the bands in the order shown. Repeat this step on the flower above, starting with the green "stem" band. Then repeat steps 5 through 8 all along the loom.

9 Insert your hook into the last peg, pick up all the loops, and gently pull the bracelet off the loom. Thread the loops on the hook onto a C-clip and attach to the start of the bracelet to complete.

Ladybug bracelet

SKILL LEVEL ✳ ✳ ✳

You Will Need

Loom

9 green bands

24 yellow bands

6 orange bands

21 red bands

10 black bands

Hook

C-clip

1 Follow step 1 of the bee bracelet, using yellow bands instead of red ones and orange bands instead of pink ones.

2 To make the ladybug, lay out red and black bands in the order shown, using two red bands for the horizontal triangle in move 9.

3 Repeat steps 1 and 2 twice more, then twist a black band four times around the top central peg to make a cap band.

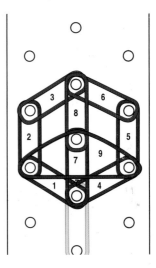

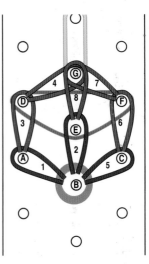

4 Turn the loom around so that the inverted end is facing you. Insert your hook into peg B and hook the black bands onto their opposing pegs in the order shown. Repeat with the red bands, using the picture as a guide.

5 Hook the rest of the loom, following step 8 of the bee bracelet. To complete the bracelet, follow step 9 of the bee bracelet.

chapter 3

awesome accessories

ladder key fob

Rubber band braids make fantastic key fobs and this simple ladder design with letter beads means you can make personalized key fobs for all your friends and family.

SKILL LEVEL ✳

You Will Need

Loom

12 turquoise bands

8 orange bands

8 green bands

10 white bands

Plastic letter beads

Hook

Split ring

LOOM SET-UP

Set up your loom in the diagonal format—3 pegs wide x 13 pegs long (see page 10).

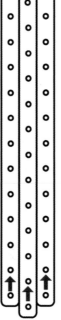

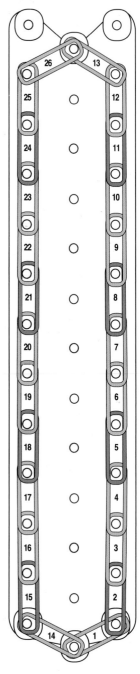

1 With the pointed end of the loom facing you, starting with a turquoise band, lay the bands over the pegs on the right-hand side of the loom in the order and color sequence shown. Repeat on the left-hand side of the loom.

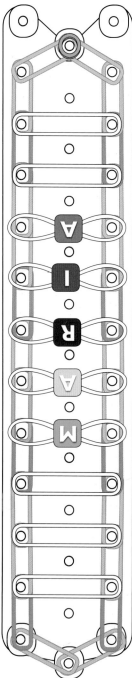

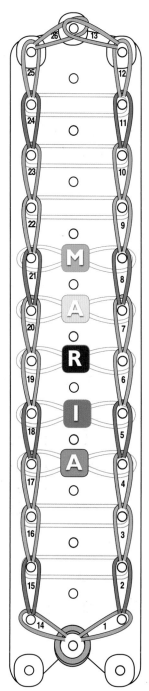

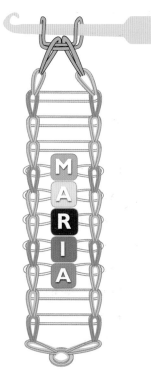

4 Insert the hook into the top peg and through all the bands. Gently pull the key fob off the loom, with the hook still through the bands. Then take another turquoise band and pull it through the loops on your hook.

5 To complete your key fob, thread a metal split ring through the loops on the hook.

2 Thread your letter beads onto white bands and then loop them over the horizontal sets of pegs. They should look upside down at this point. If you want to have a space between two words, just loop an empty white band. Twist a turquoise band four times around the top peg to make a cap band.

3 Turn the loom around so that the inverted end is facing you. Insert your hook into the bottom peg, then hook the top turquoise band (underneath the cap band) up and over its opposing peg. Then move up the right-hand side of the loom hooking all the bands over their opposing pegs. Repeat on the left-hand side of the loom.

ladder key fob 95

three-point fishtail headband

Use this simple technique to personalize and cover a plastic hair band!

You Will Need

Loom

27 blue bands

12 pink bands

24 yellow bands

24 purple bands

24 green bands

27 orange bands

Hook

2 locking C-Clips

Headband, approx. ⅛ in. (4 mm) wide

LOOM SET-UP

Set up your loom in the diagonal format—3 pegs wide x 13 pegs long (see page 10).

1 Start with the inverted end of the loom facing you. Take three blue bands, twist each one into a figure-eight, and hook over the bottom right pegs of the loom in a triangle shape, in the order shown.

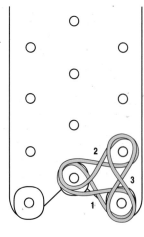

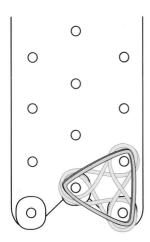 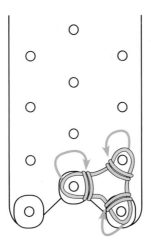 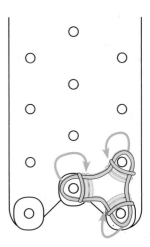

2 Loop two more blue bands over the three pegs of the triangle as shown.

3 Using the hook, take the bottom two bands on a peg and loop them from the outside edge of the peg over the top and in toward the center of the triangle. Repeat on the other two pegs.

4 Add another blue band over the three pegs of the triangle, and then loop the bottom band on a peg over the top of the peg. Repeat on the other two pegs.

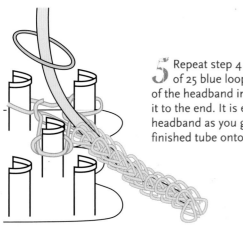

5 Repeat step 4 until there is a "tail" of 25 blue loops. Thread one end of the headband into the tail and push it to the end. It is easier to cover the headband as you go than to thread the finished tube onto the headband.

6 Now make the patterned section between the two solid areas, threading bands onto the headband and hooking them over the pegs as in step 4. Work in the following color sequence: one pink, one yellow, one blue, one pink, one yellow, one blue, one pink, 20 yellows.

7 Repeat step 6, working in the following color sequence: one pink, one purple, one yellow, one pink, one purple, one yellow, one pink, 20 purple.

8 Repeat step 6, working in the following color sequence: one pink, one green, one purple, one pink, one green, one purple, one pink, 20 green.

9 Then repeat step 6 again, working in the following color sequence: one pink, one orange, one green, one pink, one orange, one green, one pink, 25 orange.

10 To complete your headband, thread a locking C-clip through the last three orange bands and secure. You could also add a C-clip to the start of the band to stop the headband from working its way out of the tube; this makes it symmetrical, too.

three-point fishtail headband

flower hairclips

Once you have mastered these fun flower charms the uses are endless! Try sticking them to hairclips to create a cute hair accessory or gift.

SKILL LEVEL ✳ ✳

You Will Need

(to make two hairclips)

Loom

12 turquoise bands

26 orange bands

38 purple bands

Hook

2 hairclips

Glue gun and glue sticks

2 felt circles, 1 in. (2.5 cm) in diameter

LOOM SET-UP

Set up your loom in the diagonal format—3 pegs wide x 13 pegs long (see page 10).

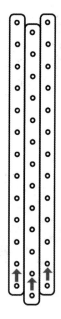

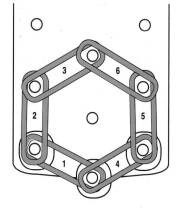

1 With the pointed end of the loom facing you, lay six turquoise bands in a hexagon shape, in the order shown.

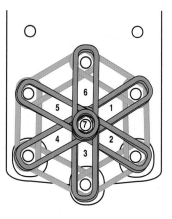

2 Working in a clockwise direction, loop two orange bands from the center peg onto each outer peg in the order shown. Twist one orange band twice around the center peg to make a cap band.

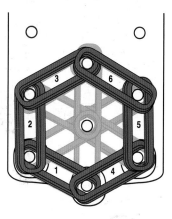

3 Following the order shown, place three purple bands on each set of pegs.

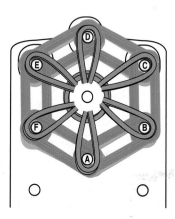

4 Turn the loom around so that the inverted end is facing you and insert your hook into the center peg. Pick up the last two orange bands added in step 2 (excluding the cap band) and hook them over peg A. Repeat, working counterclockwise from B all the way around to F.

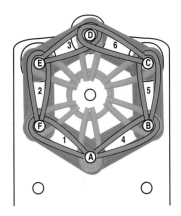

5 Insert your hook into peg A, pick up the turquoise band, and hook it over peg F. Repeat with the other turquoise bands in the order specified.

6 Insert your hook into the orange and turquoise loops on peg D (do not pick up the purple loops on that peg) and gently pull the flower off the loom. Thread a purple band through the loops on the hook and pull one of the loops through the center of the other. Pull tight to secure.

7 Repeat steps 1 through 6 to make another flower.

8 With the help of a grown-up, stick each flower onto a hairclip using a glue gun. Place a circle of felt over the back to neaten and hide the glue.

These bow charms are adorable! Show them off in your hair by attaching them to elastic hair ties with the help of a glue gun (and a grown-up)!

bow hair ties

SKILL LEVEL ✷✷

You Will Need

Loom

59 pink bands

Hook

Elastic hair tie

Glue gun and glue sticks

³⁄₈ x ³⁄₄-in. (1 x 2-cm) piece of felt

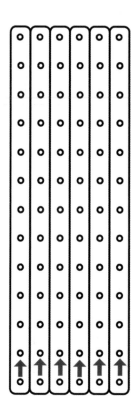

LOOM SET-UP

If you're using a store-bought loom, you will need to join three strips together to make it wide enough. Set them up in the square format—6 pegs wide x 13 pegs long (see page 8).

1 Lay the first half of the outline bands over the pegs, in the order shown.

2 To make the center of the bow, twist a pink band once and lay it diagonally over pegs B and C. Repeat with another band over pegs A and D. Lay out the rest of the bands in the order shown.

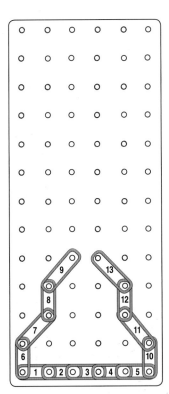

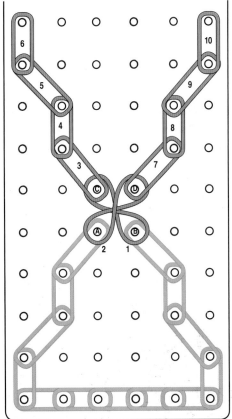

3 Fill in the outline of the bow with the rest of the bands, making sure you lay them in the order shown.

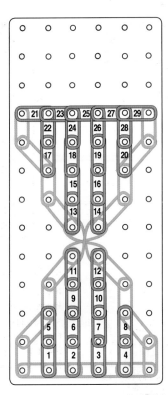

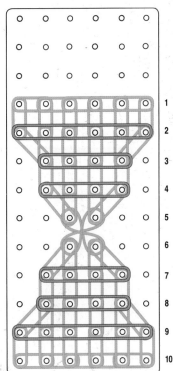

4 Stretch a band across all the pegs on rows 2, 3, 4, 7, 8, and 9.

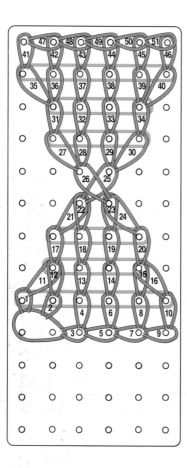

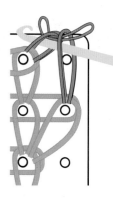

5 Turn the loom around. Before starting to hook, remove the bottom left band, twist it once into a figure-eight, and put it back on the pegs. Now hook the base of each band over the top peg that it's attached to, so that both ends of the band are on the same peg, making sure you hook them in the order shown.

6 Insert your hook into all the bands on the top right peg, stretch, and insert a pink band.

7 Then insert your hook into the band so that there are two loops on the hook, gently pull the bow off the loom, and put it to one side.

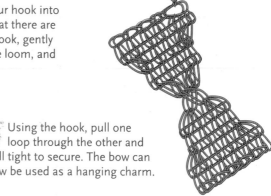

8 Using the hook, pull one loop through the other and pull tight to secure. The bow can now be used as a hanging charm.

9 To make your bow into a hair tie, insert your hook up the side of the bow, and pull the end of the hanging loop through it to hide it.

10 With the help of an adult and a glue gun, squeeze a small amount of glue onto the back of the bow and stick a hair tie onto it. To neaten the finish, glue the rectangle of felt on top.

butterfly ring

Make a butterfly charm and then attach it to a ring blank to make a stunning ring—"flutter"-ly gorgeous!

SKILL LEVEL ✱ ✱

You Will Need

4 black bands

4 orange bands

4 yellow bands

4 purple bands

Hook

Ring blank

Glue gun and glue sticks

Felt circle, $3/8$ in. (1 cm) in diameter

1 Twist a black band three times around your hook.

2 Thread two black bands through the loops on your hook.

3 Take one of the bands threaded through the loops on your hook and thread one end through the other and pull to secure. Repeat with the other band. Put to one side.

4 Repeat step 1 with an orange band and step 2 with a yellow and a purple band. Thread the yellow and purple loops onto your hook.

5 Repeat step 4 three more times, keeping all the loops on your hook.

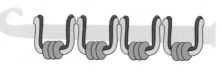

6 Take your black bands from steps 1 through 3 and pull one of the end loops through all the colored loops on your hook. Then insert your hook into the other end of the same black end loop.

7 Using your hook, pull the black loop closest to the hook handle over the loop at the tip of the hook. This secures all the "wings" of your butterfly in place.

8 Insert your hook back into the loop that was closest to the tip of your hook in step 6. Pull another black band through so that there is a loop on either side.

9 Using your hook, thread one end of the band through the other to create the butterfly's body. Pull tight to secure.

10 Cut the top loop in half and tie a knot in each end to form the antennae.

11 With the help of an adult, use a glue gun to attach the butterfly charm to the ring blank. Place the small circle of felt on the back to neaten and hide the glue.

further ideas

GLUE THE CHARM TO EARRINGS OR HAIRCLIPS OR ATTACH IT TO A HEADBAND.

cupcake earrings

Wow your friends and family with these cute cupcake earrings! Simply make your rubber-band charms and attach to metal clip-on earrings to complete.

SKILL LEVEL ✳ ✳

You Will Need

(to make two earrings)

Loom

2 red bands

2 red beads

32 pink glitter bands

30 lime-green bands

Hook

C-clip

2 clip-on earring backs

Glue gun and glue sticks

LOOM SET-UP

Set up your loom in the square format— 3 pegs wide x 13 pegs long—with the arrows pointing away from you (see page 8).

1 Thread a red bead onto a single red band and loop the band over the bottom two center pegs of your loom.

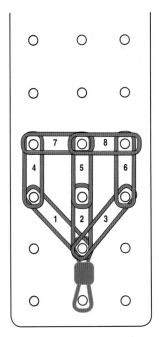

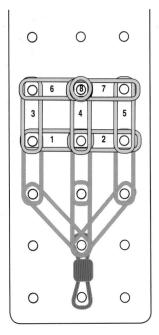

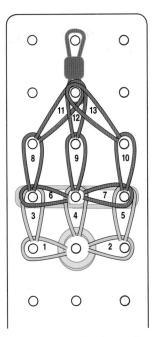

2 Loop two pink glitter bands onto each pair of pegs in the order shown: you must work in this order, otherwise the pattern won't work when you start to loop.

3 Loop two lime-green bands onto each pair of pegs as shown and then twist a final lime-green band four times around the center peg of the top row to make a cap band.

4 Turn the loom round. Starting in the center peg, insert your hook and pick up the top lime-green band (underneath the cap band) and hook over its opposing peg. Continue looping the rest of the pairs of bands over their opposing pegs in the order shown.

5 Insert your hook into the last peg and pull the single red band over the peg and through itself to trap the red bead. Pull tight and then gently pull the cupcake off the loom. Loop the long end of the red band around the red bead a few times to secure the bead and neaten the charm.

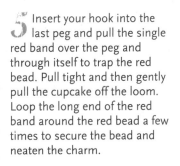

further ideas

STICK CUPCAKE CHARMS TO RING BLANKS, HAIRCLIPS, AND BRACELETS TO CREATE A JEWELRY SET.

RATHER THAN SHORTENING THE RED BAND IN STEP 5, KEEP IT LONG AND USE AS A KEY FOB OR PHONE CHARM.

6 Repeat steps 1 through 5 to make another cupcake charm.

7 With the help of an adult and using a glue gun, stick an earring back to the back of each cupcake charm. Allow to dry and cool before wearing.

loopy people key fobs

Once you have learnt to make these little people, there'll be no stopping you! Make mini family members, friends, superheroes, and more by adapting the colors and small details.

SKILL LEVEL ✳ ✳ ✳

You Will Need

(for the boy key fob)

Loom

10 black bands (hair)

26 orange bands (skin)

47 green bands (shirt)

19 bands (pants)

Hook

Keyring

LOOM SET-UP

Set up your loom in the diagonal format—3 pegs wide x 13 pegs long (see page 10).

Making the boy key fob

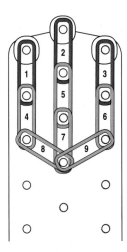

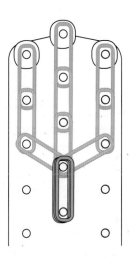

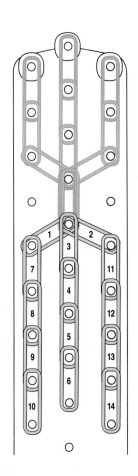

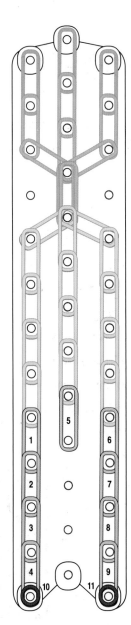

1 With the inverted end of the loom facing you, following the order shown, lay out three pairs of black bands for the hair, followed by six pairs of orange bands for the head.

2 Place three orange bands over the neck joint for extra strength.

3 Now lay out the bands for the shoulders and shirt, placing 14 pairs of green bands in the order shown.

4 Lay out nine pairs of blue bands for the pants in the order shown. Twist a black band four times around each of the two bottom pegs to make the feet.

5 To make the arms, twist an orange band around your hook three times.

6 Put two more orange bands on the tip of your hook and pull them through the first set of three loops. Then put the other ends of the orange bands on your hook so that there are four loops in total (see page 15).

7 Repeat with two orange bands to create the hand. Then add four pairs of green bands to make the shirt sleeves.

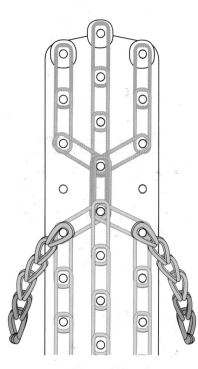

8 Place the loops on your hook on the loom peg where the shoulder is. Repeat steps 5 through 8 to make the second arm.

9 Now add one orange, three green, and one blue horizontal bands in triangle shapes, as shown. The bands on rows 1, 3, 4, and 5 should be twisted in half and used double to give the boy wide shoulders and a narrow waist.

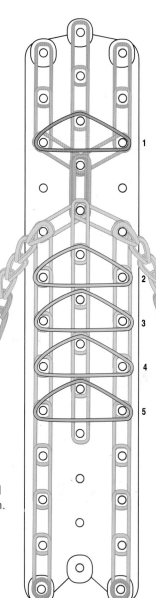

1
2
3
4
5

10 With the loom the same way as you laid the bands, not turned around, start looping the bands over their opposing pegs from the bottom upward, in the order shown.

Making the girl key fob

SKILL LEVEL ✳ ✳ ✳

You Will Need

(for the girl key fob)

Loom

20 yellow bands (hair)

30 orange bands (skin)

41 purple bands (top)

25 pink bands (skirt)

Hook

Keyring

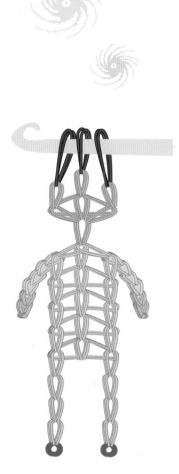

11 Insert your hook into the loops on the top peg (there will be 12 loops in total) and gently pull the figure off the loom. Thread two black bands through all the loops on the hook.

12 Thread the loops on the hook onto a keyring. If you want to make your person into a charm, thread one end of the loop through the center of the other and pull tight to secure.

Lay out the bands in the same way as the boy above, but add two pigtails extensions (made in the same way as the arms, but from three pairs of yellow bands and one pair of pink bands). To make the skirt, you have three rows of bands and three triangles of pink bands rather than one, as you did with the pants. There will only be two rows of orange leg bands before the cap band feet.

To shape the girl, place doubled-over bands in triangle shapes on rows 1, 2, 3, and 4 and undoubled ones on rows 5, 6, and 7 so that the skirt flares out. Hook and finish as for the boy key fob.

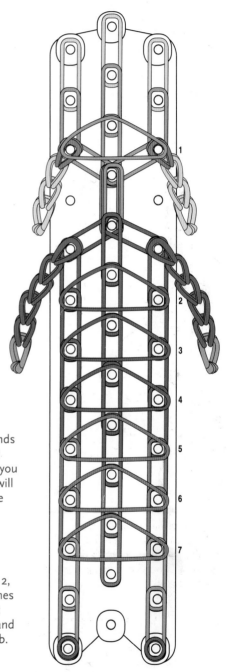

bling flower jewelry

Combine beads and bands to make this "flower power" bracelet and ring set!

SKILL LEVEL ✳ ✳

You Will Need

Loom

9 purple bands

7 yellow glitter bands

6 pink glitter beads

Hook

C-clip

LOOM SET-UP

Set up your loom in the diagonal format—3 pegs wide x 13 pegs long (see page 10).

Making the ring

1 With the pointed end of the loom facing you, lay a purple band between the first and second center pegs and another between the fourth and fifth pegs.

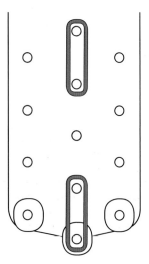

2 Lay out the remaining purple bands in a hexagonal shape, being sure to work in the order shown—otherwise the pattern won't work when you start to loop.

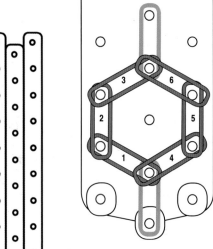

3 Thread one pink glitter bead onto each yellow band (you will have one yellow band left over) and loop the bands from the center of the hexagon outward in the order shown. Twist the remaining yellow band four times around the central peg of the hexagon to make a cap band.

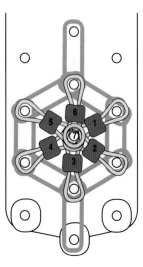

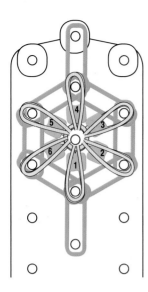

4 Turn the loom around so that the inverted end is facing you. Starting in the center peg of the hexagon, insert your hook into the top yellow band underneath the cap band and hook it over its opposing peg. Work around the hexagon in the order shown.

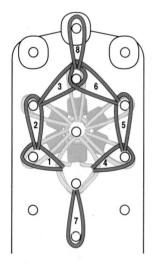

5 Now work around the edge of the hexagon, hooking the purple bands over their opposing pegs in the order shown.

6 Insert a C-clip into the bottom two loops, put your hook into the top two loops, then gently pull your ring from the loom.

7 Thread another purple band through the loops on the hook, then thread one end of this band through the other to secure. Hook this onto the C-clip to complete your ring.

Making the bracelet

SKILL LEVEL ✶✶

You Will Need

Loom

25 purple bands

7 yellow glitter bands

6 pink glitter beads

Hook

C-clip

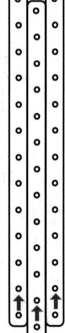

LOOM SET-UP

Set up your loom in the diagonal format—3 pegs wide x 13 pegs long (see page 10).

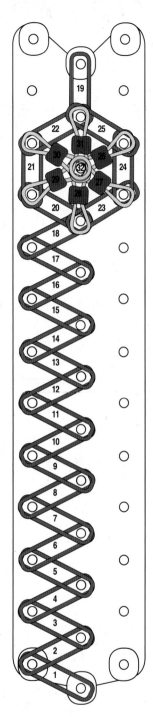

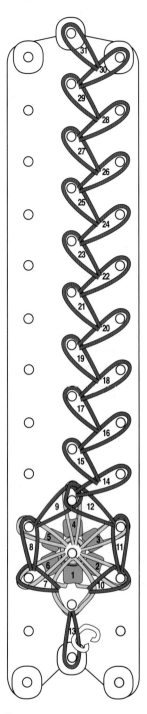

1 With the pointed end of the loom facing you, lay out the bands and beads as in steps 1 through 3 of the ring in the order shown; the zig-zag row of bands makes the wrist strap.

2 Turn the loom around so that the inverted end is facing you. Loop the bands over their opposing pegs in the order shown. Add a C-clip to the bottom two loops.

3 Insert your hook into the loops on the top peg and gently pull the bracelet off the loom, leaving it on the hook. Attach the loops on the hook to the C-clip at the other end of the bracelet to complete.

A must-loop for all dog lovers! This loopy poodle is one of the hardest projects in the book, but it's well worth the effort!

loopy poodle charm

SKILL LEVEL ✳✳✳

You Will Need

Loom

67 white bands

28 pink bands

3 black bands

3 hooks

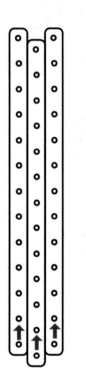

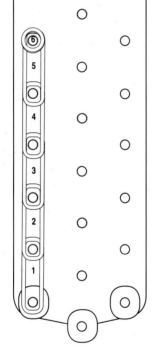

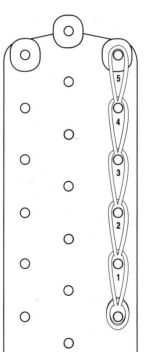

LOOM SET-UP

Set up your loom in the diagonal format—3 pegs wide x 13 pegs long (see page 10).

1 First, make the poodle's legs. With the pointed end of the loom facing you, twist five white bands in half (so that they're doubled) and place them on the loom in the order shown. Twist a white band four times around the last peg to make a cap band.

2 Turn the loom around so that the inverted end is facing you. Insert your hook into the peg with the cap band, pick up the bottom white band, and hook it over its opposing peg. Repeat all the way up the loom.

3 Insert your hook into the top peg and gently pull the leg off the loom, and place it to one side, leaving it on the hook. Repeat to make another leg, using a second hook.

4 With the inverted end of the loom facing you, place two bands between each pair of pegs in the colors and order shown. Twist a white band four times around each of the two bottom pegs to make cap bands.

5 Twist a black band four times around a hook, then thread another doubled-over black band through the center (see page 15) using the third hook.

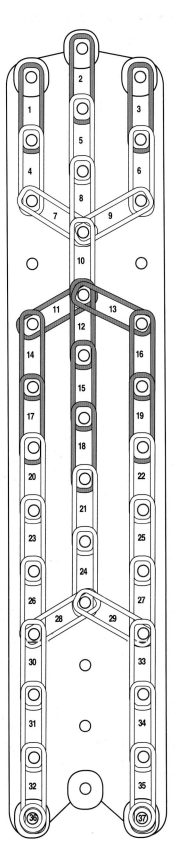

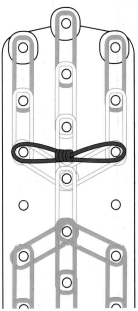

6 Place this over the pegs, three rows from the top, as shown.

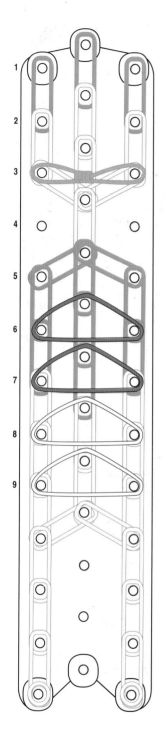

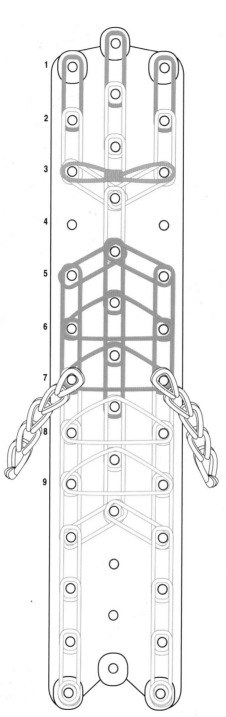

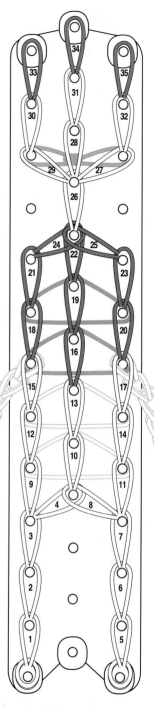

7 Place single pink bands in a triangle shape over rows 6 and 7 and doubled-over white ones on rows 8 and 9.

8 Hook the legs you made in steps 1 through 3 onto the outer pegs on row 7.

9 Insert your hook into the bottom left peg and then loop the bands over the opposing pegs in the order shown.

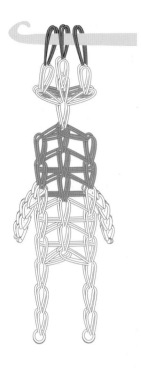

10 Insert your hook into the loops on the top three pegs and gently pull the poodle off the loom, leaving it on the hook. Insert a pink band through the loops on the hook, then thread one end of the loop through the other and pull tight to secure. Pull at the legs to shape them into a sitting poodle shape.

11 Tie a knot in the center of a black band. Insert your hook into the center loops at the back of the poodle's head, then pull the black band through these loops.

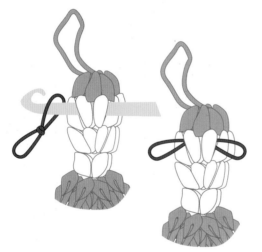

12 Turn the head around and pull the loop ends through to the front of the face to make eyes.

13 To make the ears and tail, twist a pink band around a hook four times, pull a single white band through, and thread one end of the band through the other to secure. Make two more in the same way.

14 Insert your hook into the area you want to attach the ears and tail, pull the long end through, and loop it over the pink bobble. Pull tight to secure.

loopy purse

Once you have mastered bracelets and charms, why not try a bigger project such as this purse? It would be ideal for keeping your treasures safe.

SKILL LEVEL ✱ ✱ ✱

You Will Need

Loom

400 blue bands

350 purple bands

Hook

LOOM SET-UP

Your loom needs to be at least 12 pegs long and turned so that it runs horizontally, with the arrow pointing from left to right. You will only use one strip of the loom, but it is best to use a loom that is 3 pegs wide to stop it from falling over when you are working.

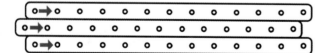

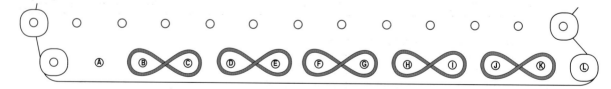

1 Twist two purple bands into a figure-eight and place them between pegs B and C. Repeat on pegs D and E, F and G, H and I, and J and K.

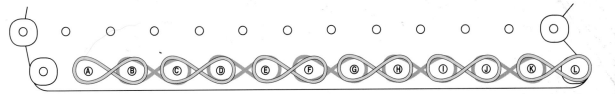

2 Twist two blue bands into a figure-eight and place between pegs A and B. Repeat on pegs C and D, E and F, G and H, I and J, and K and L.

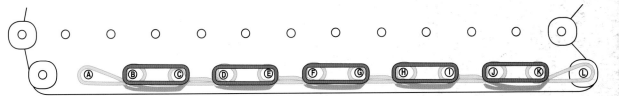

3 Starting on peg B, pick up the bottom two purple bands with your hook and hook them forward over peg B (see step 3 of the Dragon-scale Bracelet on page 52). Hook the remaining purple bands on pegs C through K in the same way.

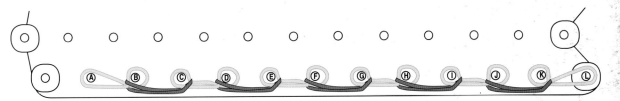

4 Lay two untwisted purple bands over the same pegs that you laid twisted purple bands over in step 1. Starting on peg B, pick up the bottom two blue bands and hook them forward over peg B. Hook the remaining blue bands on pegs C through K in the same way.

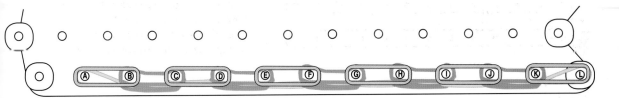

5 Lay two untwisted blue bands over the same pegs that you laid twisted blue bands over in step 2. Starting on peg A, pick up the bottom two blue bands and hook them forward over peg A. Hook the remaining purple bands on pegs B through K in the same way. Hook the bottom two blue bands forward on peg L in the same way.

6 Repeat steps 4 and 5 27 times more.

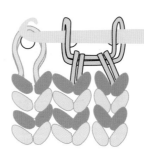

I J K

7 To take the bag off the loom, insert your hook into the loops on pegs K and L and pull them off the loom.

8 Thread a turquoise band through the loops on the two top right-hand pegs on your loom. Thread one end of the turquoise band through the other and pull tight to secure.

9 Repeat step 8 all the way along the loom.

10 Starting on the right-hand side of the bag, thread the securing loop onto your hook and then insert your hook into the four loops that are secured by that band. Insert your hook through the next securing loop of the bag and pull it though all the loops on your hook.

11 Repeat step 10 along the whole row. On the last loop, repeat the threading and pulling through of the securing loop three times to secure it fully.

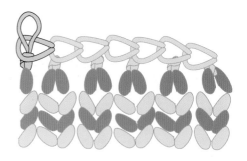

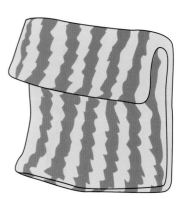

12 Fold up the bottom 4 in. (10 cm) of the purse, leaving about 2½ in. (6 cm) for the flap.

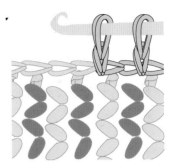

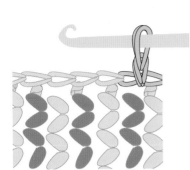
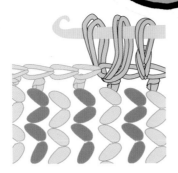

13 Insert your hook into the side loops of the folded-over section of the purse and thread two bands onto your hook. Pull the bands through the loops and thread one end of the bands through the center of the others.

14 Insert your hook with the pair of loops on it into the next pair of side loops, thread another two bands onto your hook, and pull the bands through the side loops, as before. You should now have three pairs of loops on your hook.

15 Pull the pair of loops closest to the tip of the hook, through the next pair of loops and pull tight to secure. You should now have two pairs of loops on your hook.

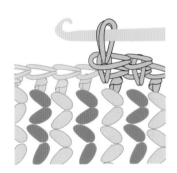

16 Pull the loops closest to the tip of the hook through the other loops. You should now have one pair of loops on your hook.

17 Repeat steps 14 through 16 along the whole side of the purse. Insert your hook along the side "seam" and pull the final securing loop through the seam to hide it. Repeat on the other side of the purse.

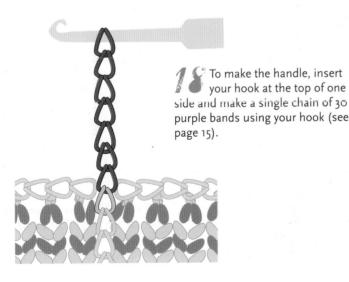

18 To make the handle, insert your hook at the top of one side and make a single chain of 30 purple bands using your hook (see page 15).

19 Once your handle is long enough, insert the hook with the loops on it through the other side of the bag. Thread a single band through all the loops and then thread one end of the band through the other and pull tight to secure. Thread the loop through the seams of the bag to complete.

circles watch strap

When you have a wrist full of rubber-band bracelets, what do you do next?
Make a watch strap out of them, that's what! Try making it with this
circles pattern—sure to brighten up any day.

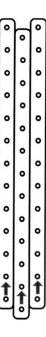

LOOM SET-UP

Set up your loom
in the diagonal
format—3 pegs
wide x 13 pegs
long (see page 10).

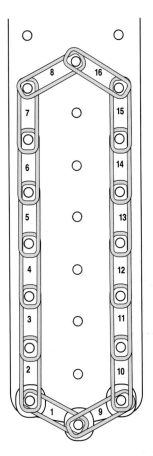

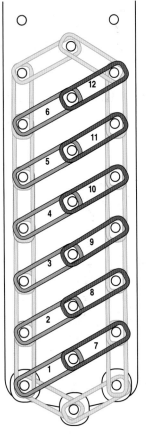

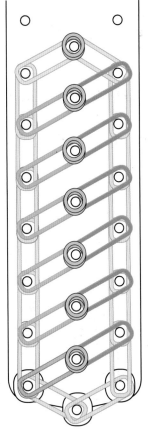

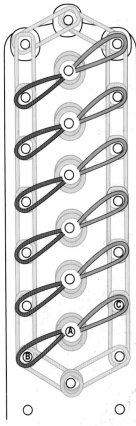

1 With the pointed end of the loom facing you, lay out 16 yellow bands in the order shown.

2 Lay six orange bands diagonally from the center pegs to the pegs on the left-hand side of the loom. Repeat with six purple bands on the right-hand side.

3 Twist a turquoise band once around each center peg except the bottom one to make a cap band.

4 Turn the loom around so that the inverted end is facing you. Insert your hook into the second center peg from the bottom (peg A), pick up the purple band, and hook it over peg B. Repeat with the orange band, hooking it from peg A over peg C. Repeat all the way up the loom.

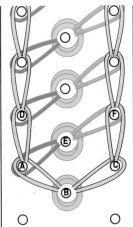

5 Go back to the bottom of the loom and hook all the yellow bands over their opposing pegs, working along the left side first and then the right side. So go into peg B, pick up the top yellow band, and hook it over peg A, then go into peg A and hook the bottom band over peg D, and so on.

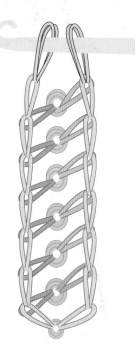

6 Insert your hook through all the loops on the top peg and gently pull the watch strap off the loom, leaving it on the hook. Put it to one side.

7 Repeat steps 1 through 6 to make the other half of the watch strap.

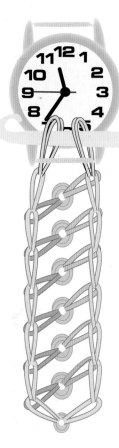

8 Thread the four loops on the hook through the slot in the watch face, then thread the loops back onto the hoop.

9 Then thread the watch strap through the loops to secure.

10 Repeat steps 8 and 9 with the other half of the watch strap.

11 Thread a C-clip through the cap band loops on each half of the watch strap to complete.

Index

Suppliers

The materials you'll need to make the projects in this book are readily available. Some suppliers are listed below.

A. C. Moore (US)
www.acmoore.com

Amazon (US/UK)
www.amazon.com
www.amazon.co.uk

Argos (UK)
www.argos.co.uk

Claire's Accessories (US/UK)
www.claires.com
www.claires.co.uk

Hobbycraft (UK)
www.hobbycraft.co.uk

Hobbylobby (US)
www.hobbylobby.com

Michaels (US/Canada)
www.michaels.com

Stuff 4 Crafts (US/Canada)
www.stuff4crafts.com

Tesco (UK)
www.tesco.com

Toys'R'Us (US/UK)
www.toysrus.com
www.toysrus.co.uk

Walmart (US)
www.walmart.com

The Works (UK)
www.theworks.co.uk

Acknowledgments

Thank you so much to Carmel, Penny, and everyone else at CICO Books for approaching me with another exciting title—it was really fun learning a new skill and having the challenge of teaching it to other people.

Huge thanks must also go to the editor, Sarah, illustrator, Louise, and designer, Alison, who worked their socks off to get this book created in a very short time frame before I went off on my honeymoon! You all did amazingly—thank you so much. It was really enjoyable and lovely working with you. I think we did a pretty good job, don't you? I hope we can work together again in the future.

I would also like to thank my new husband, Jamie, for sorting out my loops into colors—it was very helpful! You were right ... as usual...!

Finally, I would like to thank and dedicate this book to both of our families for the constant support and love that they have given us, especially over the last year. We wouldn't be where we are without you. Thank you from the bottom of our hearts.